THE CORPORATE MATCHMAKER

CREATING A ROBUST BOARD ROOM

Martin Rowinski

Foreword by Mark A. Pfister

Ultimate Publishing House

Copyright © 2021 by Ultimate Publishing House
Corporate Matchmaker
Creating a Robust Boardroom
By Martin Rowinski

All rights reserved as this book may not be reproduced in whole or in part, by any means, without written consent of the publisher.
For permission requests, write to the publisher, addressed "Attention: Permissions Coordinator" at the address below:

THE ULTIMATE PUBLISHING HOUSE (UPH)

Canadian Office: 205 Glen Shields Avenue
Toronto, Ontario,
Canada L4K 2B0
Telephone: 647-883-1758

CorporateMatchmakerBook.com
www.ultimatepublishinghouse.com
E-mail: info@ultimatepublishinghouse.com

Quantity discounts are available on bulk purchases of this book for reselling, educational purposes, subscription incentives, gifts, sponsorship, or fundraising. Unique books or book excerpts can also be fashioned to suit special needs such as private labeling with your logo on the cover and a message from or a message printed on the second page of the book.

For more information, please contact our Special Sales Department at Ultimate Publishing House. Orders for college textbook or course adoption use.
Please contact Ultimate Publishing House Tel: 647-883-1758

Corporate Matchmaker-By Martin Rowinski

ISBN: 978-1-7354831-2-2

THE CORPORATE MATCHMAKER

CREATING A ROBUST BOARD ROOM

MARTIN ROWINSKI
Foreword by Mark A. Pfister

DEDICATION

To my wife Emmy and children Daren and Samantha.

To all the Executives that I have met and ones I will meet in the future, let's build bigger ideas together through the Mastermind Group, one positive influential brick at a time!

FOREWORD

We all know that behind every successful person there were previous struggles. Likely numerous struggles, too many to count. This is, after all, what forms the drive and grit of these extraordinary people. For entrepreneurs, this is commonly a requirement and a *rite of passage* that prepares them for their impending and upcoming success. Success can also bring additional challenges, but previous struggles act as the reference point and a foundation of maturity to overcome these new challenges with effectiveness, efficiency, and with any luck, grace. This is why it is so fitting that Martin Rowinski dedicates his first chapter, The Forming Of My Drive, to kickstart a transparent look into experiences that made him who he is today and the motivations behind his work. Growing up in Poland in the 1970s, within the constraints of a communist culture, will surely give you a different understanding of surviving vs. thriving as well as the future ability to positively leverage every opportunity available to you when they arise – without hesitation. As I commonly state, *"struggles build character."* Martin succinctly summarizes this *'think and you shall become'* mantra in his writing.

From my first conversation with Martin, I knew we would not only be lifelong colleagues in the Board vertical, but also lifelong friends. His statement in the book, *"all great relationships begin with a first encounter,"* deeply resonated with me as this is a great analogy to our relationship. I had seen an ad for Boardsi and decided to check out the website. In all honesty, if the company name didn't have the word *'Board'* in it, I likely would have moved on to a different pressing task. I am glad I clicked. Finding a modern and reimagined approach to Board Director and Board Advisor appointments was extremely refreshing and led to me sending Martin an introduction email. That led to a call, and then more meetings. I am sure there will be many things we collaborate on in the future.

To summarize this extraordinary book, and to hopefully motivate you to read it cover to cover (as a great foreword should do!), think of the phrase *"unique perspective."* All too often today we are bombarded by regurgitated information that lacks innovation and is simply restating already-known concepts and ideas. These approaches do nothing to elevate our thinking nor inspire us to become better. Martin, on the other hand, is a true innovator and his teachings as well as real-life examples in this book cleverly challenge you to rethink what you have previously heard, learned, or applied. Deeply looking at the Board through a CEO's eyes is a great example. Just because the Board feels they are adding value doesn't mean the CEO sees it the same way. In many cases, it is quite the opposite. Boardsi has implemented a unique approach that flips the commonly accepted model on its head – and it makes sense!

I hope you, too, enjoy the enthusiastic style that Martin brings to the modern Board recruitment and placement industry, as I did. *The Corporate Matchmaker* has once again solidified my faith in the belief that Boards can truly make a difference in not only changing their served organizations for the better, but also elevate society on a global level.

Mark A. Pfister
CEO & Chief Board Consultant
M. A. Pfister Strategy Group

ACKNOWLEDGMENTS

Dream BIG! Without dreams no one can achieve greatness. Yet DREAMS need a lot of work in order to build the mission, vision, and values to support it. Next, finding and building a Mastermind Group that supports the DREAM is what will make the dream a REALITY!

I give gratitude and thanks to God! My family and close friends who have always been there for me through the ups and downs. Without their support through my years of entrepreneurship I would not be where I am today.

For mom and her courage to come across the world and bring me to the land of freedom and opportunities. She passed away in 2020 however the courage and wisdom she embodied which I was particularly exposed to when I was ten years old, will never be forgotten. My mothers legacy lives on through me.

To my wife Emmy, my best friend who has always been there for me, especially through the startup phases of the business, pushing me and encouraging me to keep going.

To my kids, Daren and Samantha, who have not only seen but lived as a family, at times, despite the struggles. Through it all, they smiled and supported me.

To my friends and business partners, Daniel Henry, Cameron Henry, and Richard Teal. One for all and all for one!

To my close friends and road bike brothers, Kris Baxter, Ron Simms, and Chris Bertram. We always count on each other, support each other. Just like on a bike ride when we hit hard hills, we encourage each other and push forward, and the same goes for life!

To all the executives I have met through Boardsi and many hours spent on the phone with them, thank you for your support and your advice! Special ones I need to mention, that really pushed me to write this book: Mark A. Pfister (your book really encouraged me) and Ben Nowlan from Shaparancy, what a seamless powerful partnership between Boardsi and Shaparancy!

I can write forever and thank so many people, so if you are reading this and are not mentioned, well then THANK YOU (insert name here) for everything,

No matter what others might think about your abilities, never let yourself doubt that you can do what you DREAM. You can increase your self-confidence in every way, use the power of self-suggestion, then build your Board of Advisors/Board of Directors, your Mastermind Group and DREAM big together!

Thank you to my publisher Ultimate Publishing House (UPH) for their incredible creativity and intellectual property creation for my book and journal. Felicia Pizzonia, Sofia, Roger, and the entire team is truly incredible.

I am truly blessed to be surrounded with so much love from my family and friends. Love you all!

TABLE OF CONTENTS

The Forming of My Drive 5
Restricted and Defiant 9
The Italian Outcast 10
The Making of an American 11
The Dog Days of High School 13
All Great Change Starts with a Joke 15
Boardsi and A Mission 18
I Just Wanted You to Know.... 20
1 || Why Organizations Need a Mastermind Board . . 23
How a CEO Defines an Ideal Board Member. 25
The Questions That Always Arise 26
Contributors Wanted 28
Essential Characteristics 29
The Big "D" is Diversity. 33
The Great Diversity Challenge 35
Ovation Case Study 36
The Matchmaker Highlights 381
2 || The Ultimate Date: The CEO and the Board . . . 41
How to Get an Investor to Part with Their Money 43
Change Without Warning. 45
Great Boards Complement Greater CEOs 46
The Onboarding Process 48
The CEO's Best Approach to Board Building 51

The 4 Quotients 52
A Boards-Eye View. 57
The InstaSteam Case Study 58
The Matchmaker Highlights 59

3 || A Board to Grow Serious With. 61
Expertise is Essential 63
Experience Speaks. 66
Certified for the Job 68
Diversity Unites 71
Generational Diversity 75
The Tinybeans Case Study 77
The Matchmaker Highlights 78

4 || Seeking Matchmaker to Find Qualified Candidates 81
Business Seeking Board Member 82
Future Board Members Wanted 85
Your Due Diligence in the Process. 87
Patience for the Process 93
FanWide: A Case Study 96
The Matchmaker Highlights 98

5 || Let's Make it Official. 101
Bringing an Advisor into Your Organization 102
Considerations to Document 104
The Terms of Service 105
Compensation 106
Compensation Scenario for member of Board of Advisors. . 107
Notifications 108
Intellectual Property 110
One Last Thought.... 110
Welcome to the Board. 111
Let's Talk Term Limits 112
A Critical Need. 114
Financial Compensation 115
Negotiations 117

A Story of "Conditions"........................ 118
What the Contract Looks Like.................. 119
Proprietary Information; Work Product; Non-Disclosure... 119
Miscellaneous................................. 122
Exhibit A to Advisory Board Agreement 124
Board Member Contract 125
Diversys Case Study........................... 127
The Matchmaker Highlights 128

6 || The Art of Communication 131
Be Forthright and Direct 132
Be Proactive 135
Develop Personal Relationships 136
Understand No One is Always Right or Wrong ... 137
Communication Standards...................... 138
Be a Good Advocate........................... 141
Know Your Price.............................. 142
Find an Effective Strategy 143
Viveka Case Study............................ 145
The Matchmaker Highlights 147

7 || Building Better Futures................. 149
The Critical Task............................. 151
The Factor of "Adding Value" 152
Robust Results 152
Community Involvement....................... 153
The Value, Vision, and Mission are Clearly Known ... 156
A Case Study for a Fintech IPO 157
The Matchmaker Highlights 159
The Matchmaker's Invitation 161
Challenge Yourself............................ 162
A Starting Point from the Corporate Matchmaker ... 164

THE FORMING OF MY DRIVE

Take the attitude of a student, never be too big to ask questions, never know too much to learn something new.

OG MANDINO

Looking at who I am today and my entire journey, I am certain it played a more immense role in who I have become than I could ever specifically define. Coming from a communist country tends to give a person a different perspective on life.

I was born in Poland in 1971, which was a time when the country was full-blown communist, which meant it came along with all those rules and edicts that define this type of society. After World War II, Russia took advantage of us and its people were a determined and fiery force with the goal of convincing us that being like them was best for us. We only needed to shut up and listen, and we would surely agree. Maybe others did but I never accepted that message as one I would submissively follow.

So, my small family of four—my parents, sister, and me—with my dad barely ever present, lived within these constricts the best we could. Dad was not around often because he traveled for work and was gone more than he was around, and when he was home our father/son relationship had a stronger focus on why we were so different than anything we might have had in common. Naturally, this impacted me and more than a time or two I wondered why I could not have the same warm memories of Dad that my sister had. But she was eleven years older than me...and I was the great surprise of '71.

Mom was who I relied on and she was mostly the only parent I had. Her life was tough, yet she was a resilient and resourceful woman, from the way she used our ration coupons masterfully to the ways she found to connect with me and try to build me up into a respectable character. It was through her I witnessed the first acts of negotiation in my life. One lesson I learned was that you do not need gas ration coupons when you do not even own a car, which we did not. Mom had a network of people she could trade our gas ration coupons with, exchanging them for food coupons and other needs. My sister had already moved to Italy by this time, so it was mostly just the two of us.

I still recall those days well. I was about seven years old, and I would have to go to the store and stand in line incredibly early in the morning. Waiting could be costly for two reasons. First, there were frequently adults fighting around me because times were always tense, and for many, quite unhappy. I was terrified at times, jumping out of the way from becoming entangled with a conflict. Then Mom would get there, and we would enter the store when it was our turn. This was sometimes the second reason for the wait being costly. At times, the shelves had food on them; other times the shelves were empty. Then there were times when Mom had to deal with having me, one of the pickiest eaters in Poland. Those were the days when I would rather starve that day than eat what was in front of me.

When there was no food to be purchased with our rations, Mom would have to find a way to make whatever we needed to have happen, happen. She always did and that was one of the many reasons I grew to admire her so much. Even at the time, given my young age, I knew I was fortunate to have her looking out for me. She made the difference between being hungry or not. And we never went without having at least enough food to prevent hunger. We also had the good fortune of having relatives that lived on a farm. It was pretty far away so we could not get there often but when we did, they helped us out by giving us food.

As I grew older, not having to struggle for basic needs such as food allowed me to worry about other things. Mom trusted me and that helped a lot with what I wanted to do and the freedoms I could experience within the constraints of a communist culture.

RESTRICTED AND DEFIANT

When I was a kid, we did not have to be restricted from going out and about the way kids have it today. In the United States, it was a time when a kid could go out and play all day, coming home at night and then doing it all over again the following day. Or after school if it was during the school year. Without a doubt, my arch nemesis was school. It got to me the most.

About the time I was eight years old, a new rule had been put into place regarding education. We were being mandated to learn Russian as our second language. Well, I had a thing or two to say about that and I let my teachers know I disapproved. My resistance to the very idea of learning a language I did not want to know in order to blend into a system I despised led to a personal rebellion of sorts. I became quite defiant about it. The teacher's hands were tied so they did what was the only logical thing they could do—call my mom to come down to the school for a visit.

As they told her I was unwilling to learn Russian I countered with the fact that I had enough challenges with mastering my native language in the classroom. (Okay, I did not say it exactly like that.) Mom could tell that she was not going to win in this scenario unless she made some changes. She had been hearing the chatter about Solidarność—the Solidarity Movement led by Lech Wałęsa. This was the start of the talk at that time to release Poland from Russia's grip and give it freedom from communism. That appealed to me, obviously, but Mom was scared for my life and the direction it was headed and, rightly so.

Still being quite young, my mother began to figure out how she could leave the country. To test the way the system worked she organized a trip to visit my sister in Italy. She had done this a time or two before but now she had new interest in her trips and was very attentive to the process as a whole. These good faith trips back and forth made it an easier decision for the authorities to approve her taking me along on one of these trips.

Before we left, Mom showed more trust in me than she had ever had before. She said, "When we leave, we're not coming back but you can't tell anybody, because if you do, we'll get denied." I never told a soul, not even my dad. He wanted to stay in Poland, and I later found out that Mom had already been planning on getting an overseas divorce from him when the time was right. Shortly later, I said goodbye to my family and friends. It was time to leave, and I was not going to be coming back.

THE ITALIAN OUTCAST

Admittedly, our exit from Poland was strange. Not knowing about the plans my mother had to divorce my father, it was also strange that he did not want to escape his life there. Stranger to me than it apparently was to him.

Now we were in Italy and our first place of refuge was the Polish Catholic church there. I remember my mom after we settled into our room, saying, "Let's go for a walk."

Out on the streets we meandered around with new excitement. I recall walking by a fruit stand and being absolutely amazed. It was the first time I had ever seen pineapples and bananas, and there was such an abundance of those fruits, along with others.

Then Mom found a job while she got to work trying to get us a visa to enter the United States. Yes! I was so excited, but it would be a long while before I ever got to the US. Our first application was turned down. No reason was given, and Mom could not speak well enough Italian or any English to fight the decision for denial. After a bit of time passed, she almost gave up and sent us packing back to Poland. Well, me being who I was, I made a smart remark to her about it.

"Well, you can go back but I've already been out of school for eight months. There is no way I am going back. So, I'll stay here with my sister." My words were not just a ten-year-old letting off steam; they were serious. I had no real plan, but I knew one thing that was not in my plans, and that was going back to Poland. Mom tried to tell me that was not how things worked and I retaliated. "That's how it's going to have to work for me."

After getting a teasing of what the world had to offer and everything else in it, there was no way I was going to pretend it did not happen and give it up. It would be like reaching the end of the rainbow and not getting the gold! We had to go back to the embassy and re-apply. I insisted on it and while I was not certain if Mom wanted to, but my actions kind of forced her to. It turns out it was a good thing she did. The initial denial came from a person filling in for someone else on vacation. They were sporadic in their approach, having it dictated by whatever emotion overcame them in a given moment. It turns out that we had a decent case and we got approved. My mom's sister lived in the US and was allowed in because her son had a chronic condition that needed California weather. He had been quite sick for his entire life. (He is not sick anymore and is doing great!) The biggest difference between my aunt and us was that Poland gave her permission to leave; something we didn't exactly have. Okay, we never had it but there was nothing they could do about it now.

THE MAKING OF AN AMERICAN

America is so great! Just ask anyone or watch any TV show and they will tell you that. You never need to lock your car, your door, or anything. You will always be well.

We arrived with hopes all would be well, but we had challenges right from the get-go, the language barrier being the largest one. If you could speak the language and had money you could walk into any store and get what you wanted. If you did not, which we did not, you had to rely on the other great American tradition: You can have anything that you can dream about if you learn the language, set your goals, and go for it. Well, this Polish and broken Italian speaking kid was going to go for it.

The first step I had to take was to register for school and enroll in an ESL (English as a Second Language) class. They also held me back one grade because I was behind in everything else, basically not having gone to school for the past year. I could not count Italy because I just was not serious about it. Now I was serious! At least math was easy, as it was a subject Poland excelled in academically, compared to the rest of the world.

ESL classes were hard, but I was ecstatic to learn English. I felt it was a useful language to know. It was quite deliberate in its teaching approach, unlike how I learned to speak broken Italian. Kids were kind in Italy and helped me learn what I could, and I was my mom's translator in Italy, to the best of my abilities. The kids in the US were different, more likely to pick on me for the most part and less likely to befriend a kid who could not even understand their language. If only they had known what I knew: One day I would speak the language and level the field.

My willingness to learn English was helped by there being so few Polish kids, aside from the ones in my church who did not go to my school. I will never forget one of the techniques they did in my ESL class (maybe all of them; I am not sure). Aside from the standard tapes and classwork for the program, they had a kid take me around the school and point at objects, saying what they were in English. I would repeat it and we would continue on. That helped with learning some English; however, it was not a "bully deterrent."

Kids were mean, probably not because they were actually cruel. They just teased others about what they did not know. As a result, I learned the hard way about things like ABC gum (already been chewed). To top it off, I only had two outfits to wear since leaving Poland and I had undergone quite a growth spurt. I needed new clothes, which meant a rare shopping trip to a thrift store with Mom.

Little did I know the challenges my new Chic jeans would bring me. They had glitter on the back pocket and their name was no coincidence. They were "chick jeans." I learned about this when I wore them to school and got into a fight. Not started by me but nonetheless, it was the first day of school, maybe second, and I was already in trouble at the principal's office. The only thing that kept me out of trouble was that some kids stood up for me and said I did not start the fight. Moral of the story: The year 1982 was not friendly for guys in Chic jeans. Was I a trendsetter? I will leave that up to you to decide! What I know for sure is that I was mad at my mom about the situation, and I took the serious nature of the offense out on her. "How dare you put me in Chic jeans!"

Thankfully, those jeans were in the past when Mom and I moved to Oakland. She had a new husband, and I had a life in high school to begin.

THE DOG DAYS OF HIGH SCHOOL

Three truths were evident upon my move to Oakland.

1. Oakland Tech was a tough high school, filled with gang members and other unsavory characters.
2. We would not have been there if my stepdad had not lived there.
3. My stepdad dying two years after moving to Oakland threw a wrench into my life.

The best part of being in Oakland during that time was that I was another day closer to graduating high school and I had a few friends who were Polish.

After my stepdad passed away, Mom was in a tough situation. She had to find a job and it was not that easy to do. She had been doing housekeeping and was excellent at it—hard working and committed. She finally landed a job, but it was about an hour away from Oakland, in the town of Lafayette. The family that hired her did not get their ideal fit—a husband/wife team that could garden and housekeep both. And I was no gardener! Plus, Mom was dealing with an adopted son who felt the house that we had lived in should be his, despite an agreement that said Mom could live there until she passed away. This stepson wanted us out, which would have made us homeless!

I decided to talk with our neighbor at the time, who was a lawyer, and he said that someone needed to be living there to make a case that would stick in court. Mom had to work, so it was me, and for being fourteen, even I was not sure it was a great idea. But I did it, enduring the bad neighborhood to stake our claim. I speculated then and can assuredly say today that it was not worth it. I was often scared at night and would charge down the street to my friend's house in the middle of the night, just freaked out until him and his dad would come over and check everything out. Eventually, I admitted that I was fighting for something I wanted no part of. I packed up and left the house to the adopted son and moved to Lafayette.

My new high school did not have any ESL classes, so I was on my own in the regular English class. It was hard to read and write the way I should. To this day, I am thankful to one teacher, Mrs. White, who took the time to kindly critique ways to improve my papers when I turned them in. She was an ally who wanted me to succeed and that meant a lot to me and served as motivation. For other classes, I had a great friend that would read my papers and give edits for me to implement before I turned them in. I always did the work, but he helped to make it better. I even ended up with a better grade a time or two. That is when he thought he was perhaps helping me too much. At that time, it was human help or no help at all. There was no Google or Grammarly. Thankfully! These tools are nice today, but it made me stronger doing these things the way I did. I had to learn this stuff and I appreciated learning about this quality within me, as it has come in handy for my entire life.

> **When I think something is going to be super hard, I know how to dig in and find the tenacity to do it. I do not shy away.**

Procrastination was not a choice.

Graduation was a must. And I did graduate, even getting an award for my hard work and efforts. That felt so good, I admit, and it was one of the first times it meant a lot to receive validation from others. My grades were also good enough to get a small scholarship to go to a suitcase college in upstate California called Cal State Hayward.

Life grew leaps and bounds from this point on.

ALL GREAT CHANGE STARTS WITH A JOKE

Being one of the only high school graduates from Lafayette to be going to a suitcase college, not a prestigious university was my reality. Guess what? I did not care. My mom really wanted college for me and if I was going to be there, I wanted to make the most of the experience. This was my opportunity to discover, explore, expand. My mantra was: "This is my moment to become who I want to become." And every action I took was geared toward that. I learned the easiest—and arguably most fun way—to do this was to pledge a fraternity.

Some people discredit fraternities but the brotherhood a person experiences can lead to:

- Socialization skills
- Networking skills
- Lifelong friendships
- Professional opportunities

The benefits of a fraternity were all tools that I needed to further develop. All in all, I was a shy guy. The confidence I gained through this process and participation helped guide me to my first job as a telemarketer. I talked with people and engaged in a conversation with them to get their participation. In the back of my mind, I always wondered why they would want to talk with me—the guy with still kind of broken English and a very thick accent.

The way I conquered that hurdle was to create an icebreaker with a Polish joke: "I'm a very unusual Polish person. I'm actually very smart." Once the ice was broken, I could start to work on getting the leads, whether it be for mortgages, insurance, or some other financial related product. I viewed this opportunity as a way to prove my worth to the business. My hopes were that it would make me shine. It would be time well spent if it helped me conquer my ridiculous fear of talking on the phone to people, especially people in a cold calling environment.

That joke was told to people more times than I could ever recall. It worked well often enough to land me in the company of the business's top producers. The owners liked me and equally important, I liked them, so we got along quite well. Eventually, the owners came to the decision that they wanted to grow the company. To do this, they needed to acquire some new technology. Well, someone had to learn how to use the technology effectively and they offered me the chance. Twenty-two and eager to prove myself, I agreed to it without giving it much thought. It was a good fit because I was in school for Computer Information Systems (CIS), making the concept not as challenging to me as it might be for others. Furthermore, the technology they were implementing would eliminate manual dialing and replace it with computer dialing—something telemarketers can appreciate!

Within a few months the new equipment was purchased, and a whirlwind of activity ensued. Life had changed rapidly immediately, and I was insanely busy, flying out to Connecticut with one of the owners so I could go through the training and learn how to use the new "Predictive Dialer," and then bringing all the new knowledge and know-how back to California. All this was managed by me. I had better be confident and know what I was doing. A huge growth opportunity like that does not come along every day. I was grateful but more so, I was determined to embrace it—and master it.

In order to excel, I had to shine. It required being open and brave and outspoken. I had definitely grown from the guy who was afraid to talk on the phone.

My language was no longer a handicap. Actually, it was an asset. People enjoyed it. Probably because it was different, and I was a genuinely happy voice in my environment. There was also a suggestion that I looked like Val Kilmer. He was a "big deal" in the 1980s and I welcomed the exchange. Did anyone ever tell you that you look like Val Kilmer? I would just smile and then we would start a conversation.

With shy guy being mostly gone, I found that the world was my oyster. What it had to offer was mine for the taking if I worked for it. And that is what I did. I learned to put myself out there and develop relationships in the professional world that made a difference. I best enjoyed doing all these things behind the scenes. No spotlight for me. Who wanted me in it anyway? I learned one person did—my wife. She always told me that I had a voice and a purpose that was greater than being behind the scenes. So, while I may have been happy and content being in the background, it was stopping me from continued growth.

I gulped a time or two, then finally chose to listen. I stepped out of the shadow and into the light.

BOARDSI AND A MISSION

My wife said, "You know how to network, people love you, and you need to just get out there, put yourself out there." I resisted… until she won the conversation and that is when everything grew at a massive level. It did not take me too long to get there…at least it was under 50 years.

Boardsi was introduced. A company with a mission to connect the best talents for the boardroom with CEOs who want to grow successful companies. That is the overview of all the insights I am bringing to this book.

As I undertook this new task, somewhat to my surprise, the adjustments were not as challenging as I thought they would be. Except one. Like most people, I could not stand to hear my voice. It is not exciting to listen to or see myself being interviewed. What a nervous wreck I was the first time I did a podcast. Somehow, in a way I would not have the audacity to define, it went great despite my hesitation about it. I did not sound nervous, and my answers were natural and fluid—not rehearsed or preplanned. That is when I discovered the importance of the age-old wisdom of "just be yourself."

The icing on the cake was when our executives at Boardsi and members of our network listened to that podcast and really enjoyed it. People we were trying to recruit for board positions actually reached out to us and gave the ultimate compliment. *I heard what Martin said on the podcast; sign me up.* It was a giant step, second to landing on the moon but giant for me.

Podcasts were our best marketing from the get-go. I was asked to be interviewed in them frequently and they most always reached a high-impact audience. It made a real difference in how fast we were able to start to grow the vision Boardsi carried. Some people even joked that I had insight that the "i" at the end of it would someday stand for "international." And we are going international so maybe they are right. In reality, it was just a way to get a name authorized. A sort of play on Apple and their i-products.

As I grew fluid in more situations, I could more easily solve problems and have confidence in my expertise. I found that by avoiding preset expectations I was adaptable to creating something new, something positive.

The company Boardsi is a company built to work with two groups of people:

1. Boardsi to Executives
2. Boardsi to Business

As an executive or consumer, joining Boardsi creates an opportunity to be a part of an opportunity to help businesses recognize their greatest potential. This especially applies to startups and midrange companies that are struggling. We will cover all this in specifically laid out chapters, which address:

- Why companies need a board
- The CEO's role in the process of developing a board
- Characteristics and qualities to seek out in board members and directors
- The process of finding a strong candidate for a board position
- Creating the financial terms and agreement of a board member
- Effective communication's role between CEOs and the board
- All the amazing possibilities stem from a vibrant board/company relationship

By bringing people and ideas together a win-win is created. Whether you are an entrepreneur or a CEO it is time to put your ego aside, as it will destroy you. Know that you do not have to conquer the world all by yourself. It is okay to say, "I need help."

Get the help! You really only have two choices: Sit there, beat yourself up, and struggle, or take action. Action always wins!

I JUST WANTED YOU TO KNOW…

> **A man is literally what he thinks, his character being the complete sum of all his thoughts.**
>
> James Allen, As a Man Thinketh

This quote means a lot to me because it demonstrates how a man can break away from his fears and fill the mind with positive thoughts. That is an amazing way to live! However, at times it is not easy to be this person.

Life is a journey, not a destination. Failures become important to us, who we are, and who we can grow to be. My life had many moments where I failed and struggled, just as I felt sadness too. I am on my second marriage, and we have had to deal with much adversity after we lost my stepson at the tender age of seven. It was so tough for our entire family, and my two children from my first marriage took this hard. We almost didn't make it through this, but our marriage and faith did pull us through to be where we are today. In 2020, I also lost my mom—the person who helped ensure that I had the opportunities I did to be here in America and enjoy all the freedom that comes with living in this country.

We just don't know when our time is going to be up. This means we should gladly always put our best foot forward and keep doing good on this earth before we depart to our next place, having left a trail of goodness along the way. Learning from a failure is one way to do this; giving good grace and love to life is another. Then there's encouragement, which I am hoping the pages of this book deliver to you. Allow yourself to use this information to help live out your aspirations and goals, striving to be a force of good for others while fulfilling your destiny.

As you go through each of these chapters you will find a series of thought evoking questions at the end of each one. Your answers to these questions will give you pause and force you to ponder answers that lead to a better company and board. There is a companion journal to this book that will give you the space to reflect, contemplate, and write down your thoughts on these questions.

One last thing I wanted you to know:

We all have a role in this world and each of us is meant to contribute our gifts to the best of our abilities. For some, it is digging a ditch. For me, it is connecting CEOs with boards that promote a greater vision and outcome. It is all noble work if we give it the right perspective and put our best into it. We live in a world that needs people to inspire others; a world where we need teachers. Reflecting on my life, none of this just happened. It took a lot of work and my greatest joys took place in the moments where I could be the one to help someone else, especially if they are having a bad day. This applies to everything and especially my family. They are always my primary concern and if they are not doing well, I am not well until I help them feel better, get better, do better.

Do not take your life for granted. Be involved in each day with a joyful heart and a sense of purpose. This will surely take you far!

Martin.

1

WHY ORGANIZATIONS NEED A MASTERMIND BOARD

A wise board accumulates rational wisdom, embraces unconventional wisdom, and sharpens system wisdom.

PEARL ZHU

Let me begin by offering a direct and essential insight. If you are the CEO of a public company or a non-profit there is only one option when it comes to a board. You must have one! It is non-negotiable, both by law and by the efforts that a CEO takes to ensure their organization is operating the best way possible. So, if you need a board put the effort into finding one that meets your needs. As referenced in the quote above, with a strategic board you will gain wisdom in all the areas that matter to an organization. It helps to alleviate major failures and setbacks, while promoting growth through strength.

I know a thing or two about setbacks. I have failed as an entrepreneur. Thankfully, I was able to learn and grow from those experiences so I can also say that I have succeeded as an entrepreneur. Every event that has happened to me taught me a vital lesson to implement as I moved onward. I continue to learn and grow to this day, while still maintaining the heart of an entrepreneur. I get it. None of us who have ambitions and an entrepreneurial attitude can allow our failures to stop us from obtaining our dreams.

All this begins with the mindset of a company's CEO. This is the person that others look to in an organization, both with praise in good times and with a critical eye during those challenges times that the business may be going through. Whether this person runs a public or a private company, a Board of Directors or Board of Advisors is suggested. Everyone needs a sounding board of individuals with expertise to help make the massive decisions that make a business float or sink.

If you had the choice, would you rather get out of the gate running or play catch up because you were not as prepared as your competitors were? Getting out of the gate running is the only good answer! However, there are going to be challenges along the way. To put this into perspective, let's start with a few questions to determine what a company owner (likely the CEO) may be facing:

1. Do you feel you need to do everything yourself?
2. Does your current board consist of a combination similar to this: you, your wife, and a few buddies?
3. Is establishing a viable board a priority to you?

The importance you place in your board will have a direct correlation on how others view your seriousness as an organization. Especially if you are a start-up company because this means you are likely in a race to get capital. As you go through this process one question that will always surface is the one that wants to know who you have on your board. Your answer matters greatly and there is no glossing over it. If you feel the need to do everything yourself or have yourself and some relatives or friends on your board, you are demonstrating that a viable Board is not your priority.

But how do you create the best board possible? It all begins with defining it!

HOW A CEO DEFINES AN IDEAL BOARD MEMBER

If you were to ask a CEO what they thought an ideal board and board member would be like you would get a variety of answers. Yet, these answers would likely have a common thread between them on which to base your expectations of their role. What they do matters greatly because the person that a board works with most is you—the CEO. Or sometimes a COO or other high-level executive, depending on the situation. There must be a good working relationship based on respect and ability that is also beneficial to the organization's best interests.

Here is an overview of how a CEO may define this ideal board:

> **A group of individuals that help a business, regardless of its size, benefit from developing solid policies, procedures, and plans. These individuals can provide**

fresh ideas and unique perspectives within their range of talents to help grow an organization.

These individuals can also counsel and advise the CEO from an outside perspective, as well. This group of individuals is often called a Board of Advisors and they exist for both public and private companies. The nuance is that they do not have any accountability for their ideas; they are just a sounding board and resource for growth visions and solid solutions to businesses, such as logistics challenges, for example. These individuals do not brand the company or direct it in any way.

It is this definition that you should keep in mind as you begin to determine what your needs are and how to most efficiently and effectively get these needs met. As author and American Pastor Norman Vincent Peale stated: "When you expect the best you release a magnetic force in your mind which by a law of attraction tends to bring the best to you." This is a mindset that every executive and CEO can benefit from as they work toward bringing together the best board possible.

This is when the questions start coming, also. You know what you want, but now what do you do? Let us discuss the reasons why a CEO must have commitment to the process of bringing on a board that warrants they be taken seriously.

THE QUESTIONS THAT ALWAYS ARISE

You have one guy standing before you. He is a guy with a great idea, just ask him about it. If this guy said, "I just need the money to launch this product. Everything else is covered," how would you respond? Would you be like, "Great! Here's the money." Or would you have questions? After all, investing in any company has risks but a start-up has even more. If it were a sure bet, would this person even need you?

Questions like what are posed here are worth asking, which means you must demonstrate why you are prepared to run a business. Divulge what is going to give you an edge. Usually, this means starting with building your board. The sooner you do this, the better.

Make sure each board member brings a special piece to the company puzzle. This may be:

- Strategy
- Logistics
- Marketing
- Finance

These are a few examples. It will obviously depend on whether you are a company that has got some kind of a service or whether it is a product (hence logistics).

By assembling a well-known team, it makes the process of going to a venture capital group much easier. You can show them your pitch deck, which would obviously include your Board of Advisors. All this is done with greater confidence because you are better prepared.

Now you look like a company with a great service or product backed by an experienced board. Venture capitalists pay attention to these things. If you approach them ready to launch with a board in place, it becomes easier for them to write the check. If you decide to bootstrap your business, it becomes even more important to surround yourself with a Board of Advisors because you want to make sure that your money is going to grow the business.

Helping businesses CEOs meet the board members that are an asset to the organization and contribute toward its success is one of the things that my work at Boardsi involves.

CONTRIBUTORS WANTED

One of the things we do at Boardsi is called an onboarding call. This is our opportunity to ask questions to help us learn about the business of a potential client. Having these purpose-driven conversations gives us a chance to learn and listen. This usually takes place with the company CEO. At times, the answers are surprising and lead to more questions.

This discovery process is quite revealing, and it has led to CEOs admitting they had never thought about recruiting somebody with a certain expertise for their board. There could be admissions that they have not even thought about the business's future and the need for a well-thought-out board to help ensure its success. They may be thinking, I just knew I needed to find somewhere in China to produce my product. I had not even thought about distribution and the logistics of it.

By the end of these conversations two goals have been achieved:

1. The CEO understands their gaps in preparedness better
2. It is acknowledged that a board member is needed

That is when we step in to be of service. Often times, a business's need for a single board member turns in to several, because there is a need to fill all these components. The expertise that a board member brings to an organization is their signature on its success. To meet this need, we do not need empty suits, we need visionary minds who will contribute their expertise.

These contributors have a diverse set of experiences, consisting of both successes and failures, to bring to the table. Walt Disney was fired from a newspaper for a lack of creativity once upon a time. The "man behind the mouse" not creative? Most of us can agree that is not true. You can also use somebody like Thomas Edison for an example. He failed at making his light bulb work 10,000+ times. But he grew smarter with each one and eventually the light bulb worked. His invention has impacted each of our lives in a profound way. By not giving up, Disney and Edison have shown that a desire and hard work can lead to amazing things. We can also use people like Henry Ford and Andrew Carnegie for examples. What I would not have given to be able to pick any of these individual's minds on business matters. They would have made for an incredible mastermind group for a business.

Having a mastermind is key to creating a high impact board. In Napoleon Hill's ever-relevant book, Think & Grow Rich, he defined "mastermind" in this way:

> **Coordination of knowledge and effort, in a spirit of harmony, between two or more people, for the attainment of a definite purpose.**

This means we must surround ourselves with talented people who share our vision because the alignment of smart and creative minds is exponentially more powerful than just one. Ford and Carnegie had this in common. They both surrounded themselves with a group of successful people. They formed their mastermind groups (board members), and one thing is for certain—these people had something to contribute to an area they were considered an expert in. Their insights impacted entire organizations and these people were fundamental contributors to the business's overall success.

ESSENTIAL CHARACTERISTICS

PwC's Annual Corporate Directors Survey (https://www.pwc.com/us/en/services/governance-insights-center/library/annual-corporate-directors-survey.html) has gauged the views of public company directors from across the United States on a variety of corporate governance matters for more than a decade.

In 2020, 693 directors participated in their survey. The respondents represent a cross-section of companies from over a dozen industries, 75% of which have annual revenues of more than $1 billion. Seventy-six percent (76%) of the respondents were men and 24% were women. board tenure varied, but 61% of respondents have served on their board for more than five years. This survey also found:

- 37% understand their company's crisis management plans well
- 67% think climate change should have a role in strategy formation
- 34% say racial and ethnic diversity is especially important to have on their board
- 49% think a fellow director should be replaced

Simply creating a board because you need one is ineffective. You need to create a board that produces results. Now that is as effective as it is essential.

You may think, I am just going to go out and get Shaquille, put out a great advertisement with him, and then boom—success will follow. I would never say this could not happen, but it is more impossible than likely. It is true that having this type of person on your board or making them an ambassador can help. But how does it help the company, as a whole, from the top down to the bottom up? It does not. For example, how would Shaq's smiling face be beneficial to Mary who coordinates logistics? It would feel pretty irrelevant, wouldn't it?

A great board functioning like it should results in a more successful business.

Saying you want a great board is easy. Building it is more challenging because it involves more than having just a top executive. Like I already mentioned, each board member needs to bring something to the table. Boards help to keep the company:

- Strategic
- On track to its values
- In alignment with its vision
- Committed to its mission

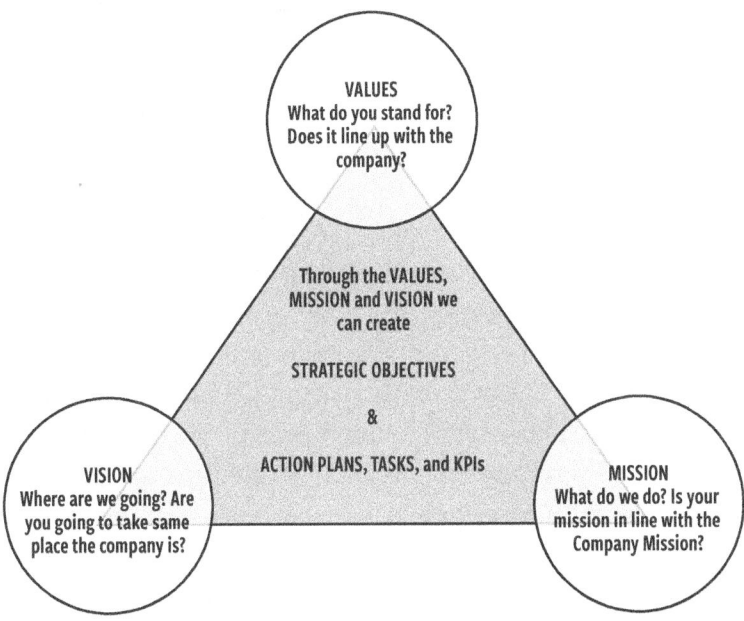

This takes place all the way from the top down, ensuring that all employees are receiving what they should be receiving. This requires a board to be:

- Respectful[1]
- Constructive[1]
- Effective[1]
- Always proactive

[1] Adapted from 'Across The Board - The Modern Architecture Behind an Effective Board of Directors,' Mark A. Pfister © March 2018 - Chapter 4: 'What Makes a Great Board?' pg. 42.

There should be a lot of focus on strategy and governance should remain result-oriented and accountable. Each member has tasks they need to deliver on in order to be effective. This includes those tasks which keep the CEO accountable, as well, while being mindful that the CEO has a lot of work to do. When all these components are in sync it leads to a dynamic board that produces great results for a company. To do this, a great amount of passion is the intangible that you either have or do not have, from day one. Because of this, no one should join a board if they are not passionate about the mission and vision a company is going to set forth.

Next, after passion is determined, a CEO can benefit by understanding the two main backgrounds of people to consider for board positions. These are:

- The individual who went straight from college into the corporate world, often referred to as a "corporate executive"
- The new executive who began as an entrepreneur

Either way, an entrepreneurial spirit has become a must for a portion of any board. The entrepreneurial spirit is what helps today's big company compete against startups. An example of how relevant this is can be witnessed from the transition from MySpace to Facebook. After Facebook surfaced, did anyone really talk about MySpace any longer? The site was quickly made irrelevant by a start up from Mark Zuckerberg and a group of guys out of a dorm room. It has changed our entire world. That is something MySpace could not have seen coming without the people on their board that understood entrepreneurial spirit and what it could lead to. Some communication about this could have went a long way in helping MySpace better understand the potential of Facebook. A person with thought processes like an entrepreneur would have had a good chance of tapping into the vision of the future.

In a constantly progressing world, this is necessary. It is as important as the last key characteristic that a CEO should desire out of a board member—and that is diversity.

THE BIG "D" IS DIVERSITY

This is from a CNBC article (https://www.cnbc.com/2020/12/15/all-sp-500-boards-have-at-least-1-woman-first-time-in-over-20-years.html): "S&P 500 companies are slowly making progress on board diversity. In 2020, S&P 500 boards appointed 413 new independent directors, with 59% of these appointments going to women and minority men, according to a new report released by Spencer Stuart, an executive search and leadership advisory firm. With these new appointments, every S&P 500 board now has at least one woman, marking the first time this has happened since Spencer Stuart started tracking this data in 1998." Diversity is essential to today's board!

To explain what diversity is to an organization is to start with what it is not. Diversity is not simply contrasting traits, such as black or white and male or female. It includes where we were raised, our educational journey, our experiences, and so on. All these things make a person's diversity shine through. What the government defines as diversity is different as we all know, they are looking for companies to place more females on boards. I agree with that; however, I also realize that you need to look at diversity a little deeper than gender, alone.

Take me as an example. On the outside, I look like your standard white male, typical board member, minus some years. Outwardly, this is me. I get it why people make assumptions; it is convenient and at times, depending on the situation, efficient. This means we are all prone to doing this. However, get to know me a bit better and there is more there.

My story adds value to my diversity. Where I came from and the consequences of the communist world that I was born into offers a narrative that is helpful to others. It is diversity of experiences and the benefits that diversity provides.

One of the biggest backlashes for a diverse board stem under the notion that there could be clashes of some sort. I am not referring to violence when I share this but differences of opinions that lead to a breakdown in communication during a board meeting. With the right people on the board, this will not happen. Board members can be diverse and have an open mind, while bringing out the benefits of their experiences. Keep in mind as you build your board, that each member should understand and have a passion for the company values, vision, and mission. When all the members are on the same page with what is important to a company, they create a common thread that unites them!

By bringing on the right people, the only angle that any individual on the board brings is their perspective on any given issue. We can learn their ideas, challenges, potential solutions, or the questions they have regarding any give topic. With the right board member, every suggestion has a basis to it. So, instead of fighting it one should research it and be open-minded about it. Maybe they just brought an idea you never even thought about before. This is what diversity brings: Strategies and ideas that may not have been previously thought of.

When Boardsi works with CEOs to start engaging with potential board members we have a specific purpose. We want to find the best people to help craft policies, decision-making, and growth decisions. This means diversity of background and experience are an essential component to creating a robust environment that brings solid governance to every level of the organization, especially if you are looking to go public.

All the decisions made in an organization ultimately have one person accountable for them—the CEO.

A board really keeps the CEO on track to make sure that these policies are created and work effectively. This makes the decisions that are made become decisions that are easy to follow so you do not harm your business. Even when you think you are doing something right, you might be harming something else. Diverse boards help you to stay in sync, predict potential concerns and problem areas, and be proactive in solutions that help a company be in its best condition possible.

THE GREAT DIVERSITY CHALLENGE

In the 2020 Corporate Board Practices in the Russell 3000 and the S&P 500 https://corpgov.law.harvard.edu/2020/10/18/corporate-board-practices-in-the-russell-3000-and-sp-500/) the reality of most Board room makeups is explained: "While progress continues to be made, hundreds of US public companies continue to have an all-male board of directors. While proxy statements may include photographs of directors, only about 10 percent of S&P 500 companies explicitly disclose individual directors' ethnicity, and 8 out of 10 of those board members are white."

Additionally, the Corporate Board Practices report had this to offer regarding the diversification of company boards: "Gender diversity has been accelerating, including among smaller companies, but female directors continue to represent less than one-fifth of the total population of board members in the Russell 3000, and 13.4 percent of Russell 3000 companies do not yet have a single woman on their board."

Prior board experience does present a picture, as noted in the Diversity Report 2017, which states: "With new skill sets now in demand, companies are increasingly looking for directors beyond the C-suite. However, they remain cautious of nominees without prior board experience." Furthermore, this report noted that boards with 3 or more women achieved 38% greater ROE.

At Boardsi, we are excited to work toward closing this gap. The component of the Big "D" is also one that is a fluid relationship between Boardsi and the individuals we bring on to train for becoming valuable board members one day. We went through an experience where there was a complaint against Boardsi that we were not embracing diversity. This hurt me to the core because not only am I passionate about it, I also serve as an Ambassador for Diversity.

This woman had been with us for five months and we had found a board that might be a good fit for her. We reached out to her because she had not logged into our platform or engaged in the correspondence we sent out. Time is of the essence in these matters, and we did attempt to reach her. If someone does not answer, how do you connect? That was the problem we were faced with. We were unable to reach her via email, LinkedIn, telephone, or any other way.

We never heard from this woman until she had someone do it on her behalf. She filed a complaint with the BBB about us, suggesting that we did not take diversity seriously. I was crushed to receive that complaint because diversity is an area that I personally take great care in and do my best to meet my own high standards for it. In time the complaint got favorably resolved but this is a situation that will always rattle me. Because it matters to me, to Boardsi, and to our mission. If you have or are building up to having an executive career with a company it should matter to you. Diversity is paramount to an effective and well-prepared organization, at all levels of involvement.

OVATION CASE STUDY

This is a success story that shows how Boardsi is committed to bringing on diverse individuals to create better boards.

About Ovation

Ovation is a customer experience and engagement platform for brick-and-mortar businesses.

Brick and Mortar (B&M) businesses often find major roadblocks when it comes to engaging with their customers. While online businesses know their happy customers and can live chat with their unhappy ones, there are 5 million B&Ms stuck with using painful receipt surveys and antiquated loyalty apps. As a result, B&Ms are getting hit hard with online negative reviews (each negative review costs a business $300-$500!) and losing billions of dollars in repeat business.

Ovation changes all of the above. Consumers interact with their simple tools in the moment that incentivize them to rate their experience and give their contact information. Then they enable business owners to turn unhappy customers into fans with an instant SMS chat feature that funnels unhappy customers away from online reviews. Their tools also turn fans into loyal customers with automated deals while prompting them to leave positive online reviews.

Ovation customers get two to three times less one-star reviews, 5-10 times more five-star reviews, and 5-10% more revenue.

Overview

Ovation partnered with Boardsi to help recruit advisors for a formal advisory board. Ovation was searching for experienced executives to help increase their reach to potential clients within their market. They were also specifically looking for executives that could increase their brand internationally in the restaurant and retail space. Ovation was concerned that conflict of interests could be a roadblock, but Boardsi was able to vet executives with no conflicts and in a timely manner. After a few interviews, Boardsi matched candidates who were the perfect fit for Ovation.

Results

Since Ovation and Boardsi partnered, the company has been able to utilize the executives' talents and are now on the fast track to branching into the international markets they were eager to get into.

Testimonial

> *"At first when I was contacted by Boardsi, I thought it sounded too good to be true, but was so intrigued, I took a meeting. I told them I wanted someone with c-suite experience in international brands in restaurant and retail, thinking it would be a tall task. In a couple of weeks, I was talking to my absolute dream advisor and was able to bring her on. It has helped my business and helped me form invaluable contacts that otherwise would have been impossible. Could not recommend Boardsi enough!"*
>
> *Zack Oates*
> *Founder & CEO*
> *Ovation*

THE MATCHMAKER HIGHLIGHTS

From a CEO or top-tier executive level, their relationship with their board is paramount to the outcomes of any company initiative. It impacts all employees from the top down. This requires an intensive effort to find board members that meet all the needs an organization has.

Use your Corporate Matchmaker Journal to write down your initial thoughts and insights revolving around these questions:

- What is my attitude about the tasks that need to be done in my business?
  - Do I feel the need to do them all?
  - Are there people I can rely on for effective brainstorming?
  - In what ways can my effectiveness improve with the right board?
- What is my personal definition of a proven board member or advisor?
- What strengths does my business offer to attract the attention of the best board members?
- What areas could my business improve upon to attract stronger board members to it?
- What are the benefits that an outside organization could bring to the process of successful recruiting for board members?
- In what ways would my company benefit by having experts in areas on a board compared to only people I am familiar with?
- What does a vibrant relationship with a board feel like it would bring to my workday and the company's ultimate success?

One final question for you to contemplate. As thinking about building out your board, knowing that Millennials make up 50% of the global workforce today, and it is expected to surge to 75% by 2025, what are your board's demographics risks at this moment?

These questions will guide you in recognizing areas of strength and weakness in how your organization is being run. It offers a great transition for what we will discuss in the next chapter, which is the CEO's role in facilitating a health relationship with board directors and advisors to an organization.

THE ULTIMATE DATE: THE CEO AND THE BOARD

Coming together is a beginning.

Keeping together is progress.

Working together is success.

HENRY FORD

All great relationships begin with a first encounter. Henry Ford understood this, and it is something I passionately believe, as well. When it comes to knowing when the right time is to create a board for a business is, the simple answer is "right now!"

The process of creating this dream board is more complex than simple, however. In my work at Boardsi we come across a lot of different businesses. We learn about some through our business development research and decide to reach out to them. At other times, these businesses reach out to us. My LinkedIn box alone is frequently filled with new opportunities someone wants me to know about. The purpose is always for them to introduce themselves to me in hopes that I can get them what they need. And I am in the business of building relationships where I can hopefully do that. However, to do this it does require me getting past the biggest question they often ask about right from the start: Martin, do you know anybody who can fund my business?

To be direct, I say something along the lines of "perhaps," the most indirect answer possible. It really depends on one thing, first and foremost, and that is the board. So, I ask about it and this is when the details start to emerge. Some people say that their board consists of them, some family members, and a friend or two. At times, people will ask why everyone is asking about if they have a board and they do not understand the significance of it. This is when I know they have approached others before me. Then there are also those people who have not started to contemplate a board yet—they are not to that point. To me, creating the board is exactly the point.

> **No matter how incredible your idea may be, venture capitalists and investors are not just going to throw money at it. Due diligence is required.**

Great ideas require great guidance and insights too. A board brings these things and as a result, CEOs thrive on the relationship they build with this group of skilled and qualified individuals. It is not just Boardsi this is important to; it matters to investors, as well. Why else would they ask about it when someone approaches them to invest in an opportunity? This is worth exploring more closely.

HOW TO GET AN INVESTOR TO PART WITH THEIR MONEY

Boards create credibility and anyone who wants to invest in a business will require the business be credible. Not everyone will explain this, and yet it is one of the most important things to explain at the onset. It helps the entire process begin to make more sense—it is logical.

Assume you are an investor with a wealth of money. You know you are going to go out and fund companies yourself. If you had two choices of the same or similar service that came to you looking for funding you would evaluate and compare the two companies against each other. One guy has built a board to support their idea and is drawing from their expertise to formulate a strong plan. The other guy plans to put these people into place after he receives funding. Who do you prefer? The guy who planned ahead to present you with a strong case for investing, or the one who wants your money so they can start the hard work? The first choice is obviously the one most (okay, all) investors would prefer.

Another thing that an investor would look to see is an exit strategy. Even when a business is just starting it is important to build it up on the premise that you will need an exit strategy. This brings up questions, with two of the most significant being:

- Are you going to grow this business and sell it?
- Are you growing this business to go public with it?

This does not mean you need the advisors for these strategies in place immediately, but these are all things that require consideration and a thoughtful plan of some sort in place. At minimal, bigger than just saying, "We plan on going public and our success will skyrocket." If someone were to say this, I would simply ask, "How?" Then we would continue the conversation.

Take a moment to envision your company as a construction project. In this scenario, your Board of Directors would be your support beams that hold the structure up. They ensure everything stays together and do not compromise their strength, which is the quality of their input to a CEO.

You should also go back to the exit strategy questions. If you are planning to go public, the next question would be: Have you taken a company public before? If you have not been part of a company that went public and in which you were deeply involved in the initiative and efforts, then bringing on a board advisor who has would become critical. For example, a CFO that has taken more than one company public can offer you an individual with a track record and a high level of support behind an exit strategy. If you plan on selling or merging, bring on a M&A expert to help you guide the company toward that goal. The people you bring to a board are what will give it the expertise that helps your business to thrive, regardless of what your goals are.

In the end, investors will look for these things at some point in their process of determining if they will invest in you, and how much. It is better to be prepared by having the board piece of the equation in place. You never know when something is going to happen that requires the expertise that a board member can bring. The year 2020 highlighted this with the onset of COVID-19.

CHANGE WITHOUT WARNING

If there is ever a situation that surprised the world it was the onset of COVID-19. It changed everything in our lives rapidly. This includes how we conduct business. In reality, there were not a lot of businesses that had a strategic plan in place for an event of this magnitude. As a result, a lot of companies were in for a rude awakening. Businesses worldwide came to a halt, leaving CEOs and their boards scrambling for solutions to minimize the disruption. It felt like a zombie apocalypse, didn't it?

Suddenly everyone was trying to figure out what they could do. Whether it was a business in an office building, or a restaurant/retail business immediate action had to be taken. In the US, alone, business was basically shut down for as little as six weeks and as much as a year plus. It was chaos!

Most boards did not have an epidemic expert on them whom they could turn to. Yet, some were able to act swiftly and put strategies in place that allowed them to maximize their impact in a positive manner. One example of this is Peloton. Their stock blew up as people started to purchase the exercise bikes for their home. Gym stocks got destroyed because people either could not go to a gym or they were not comfortable doing so. If you were either one of these businesses, how do you think your preparedness would be? Board-driven strategies are for both growth and disruption alike; Peloton was able to capitalize on the situation in a powerful way, gyms could not.

Another example is Zoom. In a flash business became virtual and Zoom instantly went from being a useful tool for business to an essential one. Their explosive growth was met with challenges they had to face and resolve quickly. Suddenly the world was looking to them and they stepped up to the plate swiftly and efficiently, a combination of insights, strategies, and specific actions that were spearheaded by the CEO, other executive staff, and the board.

These two examples of opportunity are countered by examples where people were not prepared for what COVID would bring to their business. One example of this is a woman I know who owns four boutique stores in California. With the shutdown, these stores were naturally shutdown too. The challenge was that she did not already have in place or begin to implement an eCommerce store for her business. She was struggling quickly and whether she could make it through or not was yet to be determined. This is an example where the right advisor could have worked with her to find a way to still connect with customers, even if she only wanted local customers, through the internet. Perhaps a hand-to-hand white glove kind of service. It would have been an idea to seriously ponder in order to survive.

Survival is the goal in times of crisis, isn't it? These same challenging opportunities present businesses with chances to grow exponentially, shift accordingly, or just drift away into nonexistence. The ones who have advisors and board members that know how to extract opportunity from the situation are the ones who, at minimal, will survive and preferably, thrive. CEOs rely on these people to give them the broad view while they are managing the daily operations.

GREAT BOARDS COMPLEMENT GREATER CEOS

**Stay committed to your decisions but
stay flexible in your approach.**
Tony Robbins

This quote by Tony Robbins is spot on for the way we should contemplate business. Back in the 1900s you could have a strategy for business, and it was likely to be the same across almost every type of business. The same was true basically through the 1980s. So, what changed? Technology is what changed. Today, it is impossible to be an effective CEO or board member without a sound foundation of technology. It is the ideal strength to have, along with a flexible strategy.

The best CEOs and boards come together when they demonstrate these two qualities of flexibility and strategy. It is what allows them to make shifts more quickly and this means they can take advantage of trends more swiftly, whether it is an adjustment to make money or minimize loss. Look at the COVID examples to support this.

Through the development of a strategy, you can begin to understand how you should conduct your day-to-day business, while also ensuring you are prepared to adjust quickly, when required. Regardless, the goal should be the same in the relationship between the CEO and the board.

Where you do not find a strategy, you often find misalignment. What happens when goals are misaligned? You could have a map with your line from Point A to Point B, with B being your goal. Then somebody comes along and says the goal is really at Point C, so you have to go to C now. The person is annoyed because they are almost to B. They say they are going to just keep going. The problem is that now the goal has been moved. When you get to B you are off-mark and by the time you finally reroute to C you are too late and have lost a valuable edge. Without a board and CEO being aligned, missed goals are often the result. Flexibility is the only way to prevent this from happening in your organization, most of the time if not all of the time.

The way to keep this all on track is to ensure that everyone involved understands the company's:

- Values
- Vision
- Mission

The CEO knowing these—and fully believing in all three, as written out for the company—serves as a guide to knowing who is needed for the company's board. Doing this before creating the board leads to saving wasted time on potential board members who are not aligned with the values, vision, and mission.

> **CEOs need to understand what qualities a board member will bring to the table.**

This can be harder than you think, especially if you are a start-up company. In this case, you might not have the values, vision, and mission set yet. You also may not have anyone you can talk with to explore ideas and see where your natural strengths lie and where you need to tighten things up. By working closely with people who can help you identify the missing pieces it will be much easier to find the right executives to fill in those holes.

Public companies are more likely to know what they need most of the time. Perhaps it is not the best scenario, but they have the general direction down. This is why in every case an organization like Boardsi brings advantages to a business who has a board or advisory role that needs to be filled. We go through a specific process to make sure that we are connecting compatible, growth and vision-oriented board members to CEOs. You guessed it; we are making the ideal date through what we do. The term we have for this is the onboarding process.

THE ONBOARDING PROCESS

The onboarding process is essential. During this process, we get to know what a CEOs needs are and how we can be of service in helping them to fill the gaps. If they are precise and have a clear understanding of their needs, we may even be able to make a recommendation of a few executives that we feel would be a good match. This is when we hear the light bulb come on and the conversation changes. More ideas start flowing.

The first drive to building a board is to develop the goals; short-term, mid-term, and long-term. They all must be defined, and this means that a CEO must be prepared and open to bringing on members that you never thought you would need. One example is that a business that is lacking a strategy may need to bring on an executive that understands this. This is the person that has "been there, done that."

The expert who can help you to build growth strategy might be your first board member. This is a valuable role because this person can help you to build out the rest of the board. There are times at Boardsi that we act like that first board member and plant a seed to help the company come up with the best choices to fit their needs. There are advantages to working with us, such as:

- We have a network of executives from many industries with lots of experience, expertise, and certifications.
- Finding funding—has access to a large funding network.
- Members of Boardsi have already expressed to us that they want to join a company as a board member.

We waste less time fishing in an empty pond and more time picking from ready and prepared executives that are ready to serve on a board. At times, people will tell us that they can go to LinkedIn and search out for executives. This is true; anyone can do this, and it is not a bad idea. The problem is that if you factor in your time, you are wasting a lot of it searching with no guarantees of finding the right person who also has the time to commit to your company.

Time is a major consideration for both a CEO and potential board member to be serious about. If you spend X amount of time with a few executives that you have been interviewing. They like what you have to say, and you like what they have to offer. Then it comes down to the one last detail of time. You share what you need, and they respond, "I really don't have that much time to put into this." They go on to explain all their obligations. When this happens, the CEO has wasted their time. One of the high value propositions Boardsi offers is that they already know that a potential executive they introduce to you has the time. These people have expressed that they want to help companies by bringing their talents to the board and they have committed to offering the time required to do so.

Are you wondering, how much time? The average amount of time a Board of Directors member should expect to commit to one company is 200+ hours per year. A Board of Advisors member should be prepared to commit at least 50+ hours per year. For advisors that number can be easily more or less, depending on the role and commitment that the company is expecting from the member. If you are an advisor, you can usually be of service to more organizations simultaneously.

As a CEO, you also need to consider how much time you want a board member available. You do not want to bring on an executive just because they have a famous name within the business community. For example, having Bill Gates on your board just because he is Bill Gates may bring some name recognition to your organization but what would Gates be doing for your organization? You could pay him X number of dollars and put his name up on your website, but you also need something in return. With a busy and successful guy like Bill Gates who has moved on to philanthropy, you would want to be careful. I am quite certain he is a busy guy!

As a CEO, all your moves need to be effective, or you are operating inefficiently. Creating the board is perhaps the biggest starting point.

THE CEO'S BEST APPROACH TO BOARD BUILDING

Ask yourself this question: Would I rather own a hundred percent of a million-dollar company or 10% of a hundred-million-dollar company, or even a billion-dollar company? The math is easy. The latter is better. If you prefer the first option, it is likely ego that is getting in your way and you will want to work on that. Because having a million dollars and doing everything yourself with no help is going to be stressful, if not now, at some point. Whereas having a team that helps you earn a hundred million can be less stressful, more exciting, and bring the opportunity to learn to the table. This setup creates a network that helps to plant seeds for the future and ultimately make more money at the same time.

Building a network offers so many benefits, with the obvious one being that you can build your company to a significantly higher level. Whatever you have given up will tenfold what you could have done alone. Plus, it builds a brighter future. If you own a company and have a ten-year run with it, then sell it, you did great for a few reasons:

1. You built a network of executives to have as resources if you build another business
2. Through your smart, hard work you have created opportunities to become a board member of other organizations

You have wrapped yourself around successful people that helped you arrive at where you desired to go. Now you can stay connected to your current network and also have a private network where you keep your mastermind group to bounce ideas around with. You never know what could happen next! What you can say is that you have created a win/win situation.

I am not suggesting that you should build out a board that takes 90% of your company. It does not require you to do that.

Depending on what each member brings to you, you can decide what they will be compensated with. (We do have a chapter on creating the compensation structure you will get great information from later on in this book.)

The overall objective during the process of creating the board is that the networking and interviewing CEO will understand and actively work toward finding the right team based on each individual, for starters. This goes further by also learning how these candidates work with the team, as a whole, to bring value and adhere to the vision and mission of the organization.

Now the question becomes: How can I ensure I am getting the right board members that meet the criteria of value, vision, and mission? For the answer you need to look to the four quotients.

THE 4 QUOTIENTS

Before bringing any board member on it is important to thoroughly analyze the type of person they are and how they would be an asset to the organization. To do this, it pays to look at the "4 Quotients," which are:

- Intelligence Quotient (IQ)
- Emotional Quotient (EQ)
- Mindfulness Intelligence (MQ)
- Adversity Quotient (AQ)

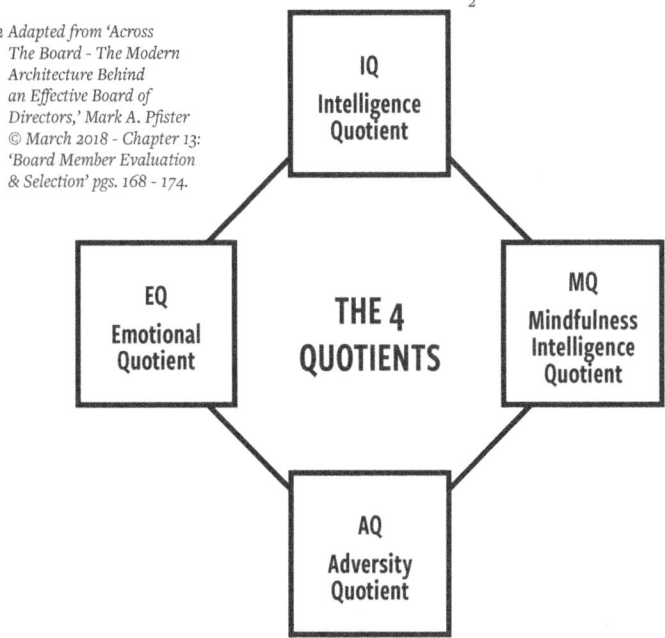

2 Adapted from 'Across The Board - The Modern Architecture Behind an Effective Board of Directors,' Mark A. Pfister © March 2018 - Chapter 13: 'Board Member Evaluation & Selection' pgs. 168 - 174.

Most of us have heard of IQ and EQ; however, all four of these quotients are important to consider when selecting board members.[2] After all, these are the people that will help to craft and carry out the policies that your organization puts in place. These people will become the diverse group of individuals that give you the complete picture. This includes diversity of gender and color, as well as other forms of diversity you may not have considered, such as:

- People with their PhD in an area of expertise your business requires
- Young and successful entrepreneur that just sold a company for a billion dollars
- Individuals who have helped to turn a company around from no profit to high profit

All these diverse experiences offer value to a business. They also drive strategic focus, prevent goal diversions, and guide the company with priorities. An effective board helps with accountability for all employees, including the CEO.

When a CEO builds trust and credibility with their board the opportunities to grow a stronger network exist and mediation, when necessary, is more easily done. All this information is the end result that following the 4 quotients will deliver.

- With IQ, we measure cognitive capacity.
- With EQ, we determine one's ability to recognize, understand, use, and manage one's emotions.
- With MQ, we look at a person's ability to gauge right from wrong, and to behave based on the value of what we believe is right.
- With AQ, we define how resilient and adaptable a person is.

There is one quality that describes AQ perfectly and that quality is grit. Not all of us possess this but if we do it is an indicator of our attitude, reactions to mental stress, perseverance, longevity, learning, and response to changes in our environment. Each one of these quotients is one that should be represented in CEOs and board members alike.

When it comes to IQ, we should always strive to keep learning because the more we learn the more opportunities we have. Ways to do this include:

- Continuing to study
- Doing something you have always wanted to do (piano lessons, for example)
- Learn a second (or third or fourth) language

I have found that IQ is also enhanced by the activities we choose to do. For me this means working out to keep the blood flow going. Really, exercise and movement help to put life and business into perspective. This is particularly beneficial when it comes to managing EQ.

> **Self-awareness, self-management, social awareness, and relationship management are an intricate part of our lives because our awareness of how we handle these things determines the quality of our outcomes.**

I am no stranger to what it is like to not handle these things well. I used to take things very personally, trying to make the world fit into my shoes and having little regard for other people's situations. If someone yelled at me or screamed at me, it impacted my mood a lot. As I grew older and became a driving teenager, aggressive drivers would cut me off. My first instinct was like many others, flip them the bird and then complain about them. I would not say these situations ruined my day, but they took away from me giving myself the best day possible. It took me awhile to understand that if I put myself in their shoes, I might better be able to understand what was happening. Most likely; this person was dealing with something and if they lashed out toward me it was about something not involving me at all.

When we take time to explore why another person may be responding the way they are to a situation, we take a step toward emotional maturity. Even if they were to punch you in the face (heaven forbid) that would likely be the result of something falling apart in their life. It would have nothing to do with you. Pause before you act or speak. It can save you a lot of hassles, trust me.

> "Words are powerful. They can be positive or negative, elevating or criticizing. Make the right choice, pause, think and then reply with positive supportive encouraging words!"
> Martin Rowinski

There once was a time when I must have liked to hear myself talk too much. I would always speak before I thought, and it got me into trouble often enough, either through asking stupid questions (those that are inappropriate) or by making a comment. As we all know it is not wise or kind to make a comment on someone else's appearance. Yet it can happen, and it does not make me happy to admit that it used to happen to me. I wasn't intentionally cruel or insensitive, but my words didn't come across as kind or compassionate. Thankfully, it is a lesson learned, albeit the hard way a time or two. God did give us two ears and one mouth for a good reason.

Part of God's reason for two ears and one mouth extends to our ability to accept constructive criticism without rushing to offense or judgment. We need to hear what other people have to say and evaluate it thoughtfully and not take it personally. When you put your feelings aside it is quite incredible what you can learn from somebody else's perspective.

> **"A particular train of thought persisted in, be it good or bad, cannot fail to produce its results on the character and circumstances. A man cannot directly choose his circumstances, but he can choose his thoughts, and so indirectly, yet surely, shape his circumstances."**
> James Allen, As a Man Thinketh

I have been criticized plenty of times in my life, either directly or through my perception, which is just as harsh. An example of this would be when someone asks for my advice and I offer it, only to learn they did not do anything with it. I take this as a form of criticism. Why did they even bother? Was it just to laugh at me or try to prove I was a fool?

Thankfully, I have come to a resolution with this type of insecurity. It does not impact me the way it used to because I do not take it personally. That does not mean that I do not value my time. No one has permission to pick my brain time and time again, just to ignore what I have said or take no action of their own. That is also emotionally intelligent, as well as a marker to one's ability to handle mature intelligence.

When we have MQ, we can distinguish right from wrong, both personally and professionally. This is pretty clear cut and guided by our moral compass. If we feel something is wrong and do it anyway, we are willingly choosing wrongly and jeopardizing having a healthy MQ.

With a robust IQ, EQ, and MQ, we will find that we possess the grit to master the AQ.

All of these qualities make CEOs excel and give a solid blueprint for what you can strive for in this position. Be the person your board needs, and they will be the people you need, in return.

A BOARDS-EYE VIEW

Although a CEO chooses the board, the board will have a profound impact on this person. It is up to the CEO to demonstrate why they are a good choice for the board. Some qualities are consistently more important than others, starting with ego.

Egos are the downfall of business, when not healthy, and CEOs must be aware of this. If part of the mission is to build a board that will be effective, the insights given should be taken seriously. Being open to advice as a company grows is important, making the choice to surround yourself with the best talents on your board or with advisors matters more. As a CEO, you want to engage with the board, take their advice and wisdom, guide the company with their input in mind.

The way this type of engagement is often done is through meetings. When you are scheduled for a meeting be on time. This is good advice for all but critical to a CEO if they want to show respect and value for their board's time, energy, and commitment to success. People who show up for a meeting on their time are revealing they have an ego that says their time matters most and you need them more than they need you. Big mistake!

Being efficient with time matters for a great many reasons. I think it is imperative for a CEO who meets with their Board or Advisors to prepare an agenda and send it out ahead of time. The more everyone is prepared the better the meeting will be.

One last thing, just as a CEO is expected to build a board that is robust in the areas of IQ, EQ, MQ, and AQ, a board should also expect these qualities of the CEO they will be aligned with. When people understand the expectations, then experience the benefits of them, great companies are established. That should be the goal.

THE INSTASTEAM CASE STUDY

With this case study, we are able to show how important it is for relationships to bring fresh and innovative ideas to the board.

About InstaSteam
InstaSteam is the world's first, electricity-free and hands-free portable steamer that steams clothes within minutes and adds to the lifespan of garments. While a regular iron smooths out wrinkles, it also crushes the fragile fibers of the textiles which causes irreparable damage to the cloth and shortens the lifespan. Ordinary steamers tend to spurt or leak water, but InstaSteam's eco-friendly mineral reaction causes water to be transformed into oxygen and hydrogen in the form of steam. InstaSteam is also the first-ever clothing steamer to be allowed on airplanes and cruise ships.

Overview
InstaSteam partnered with Boardsi to help recruit advisors for their company. They were searching for executives that could help

them branch into the hotel industry and further the distribution of their product. A few months into the recruiting process, an introduction was made between InstaSteam Founder and CEO, Ari Hirsch and Virgin Hotels CEO, Raul Leal. Shortly after, Raul was signed as an advisor for InstaSteam.

Results

Due to the connection Boardsi made between Ari Hirsch and Raul Leal, InstaSteam landed their products in multiple hotels and cruise ships and continues to increase those results. The company is now positioned to make a huge leap into an untapped market.

Testimonial

> *"Boardsi definitely exceeded my expectations. From the first phone call I had with them, they already had the ideal board member/advisor for my company. Even after I brought on my first board member with Boardsi, they are still continuing to help me make more invaluable connections that benefit my company. I would highly recommend Boardsi to any executive looking for a new opportunity or company looking to expand their business and grow their team."*
>
> *Ari Hirsch*
> *Founder and CEO*
> *InstaSteam*

THE MATCHMAKER HIGHLIGHTS

I am drawn to the way a business can operate and function when the expectations are clearly defined. This helps to fill the gaps and make sure all angles of a company's needs are addressed. To make this happen, it does require some thought about where you are, where you want to go, and how to best get there.

The questions to help you determine how the information shared in this chapter applies to you are listed below. These insights can be written, evaluated, and updated in your Matchmaker Journal.

- What is my ideal relationship with a board?
- How is my company's vision defined?
- What is my company's mission?
- How prepared is my business plan for funding?
- Is a board already in place?
- Who is on it? What experiences do they bring?
- Where are my strengths within the areas of IQ, EQ, MQ, and AQ?
- What areas could I find improvements for with IQ, EQ, MQ, and AQ?
- How does my ego impact my work and working relationships?
- If I were to have a board define me as an individual, what would they say?

These questions have all offered insights into the reality of what your current situation is, as well as what your strengths and challenges may be. Your honest assessment of these things is a perfect transition into our next topic, which has to do with the characteristics and qualities of excellent board members. These are the individuals who will fill the gaps that you require to be a successful CEO.

3

A BOARD TO GROW SERIOUS WITH

To succeed as a team is to hold all of the members accountable for their expertise.

MITCH CAPLAN

Every CEO has their own set of hopes and expectations that they would appreciate seeing in their board members. If these needs were met, we'd feel like we'd struck gold. The challenge is this: How are these needs determined? A team's success is something each person on the board is accountable for in some capacity. Their expertise is meant to be a positive force for better results.

There are four criteria that need to be factored in for creating a dynamic board that serves a company and its best interests well. At Boardsi, we do get it! We know how frustrating this could be and work diligently with companies to get the formula right. In order to prepare the right board members to take on roles with organizations to be of service to we have developed a four-quadrant approach to gauging readiness.

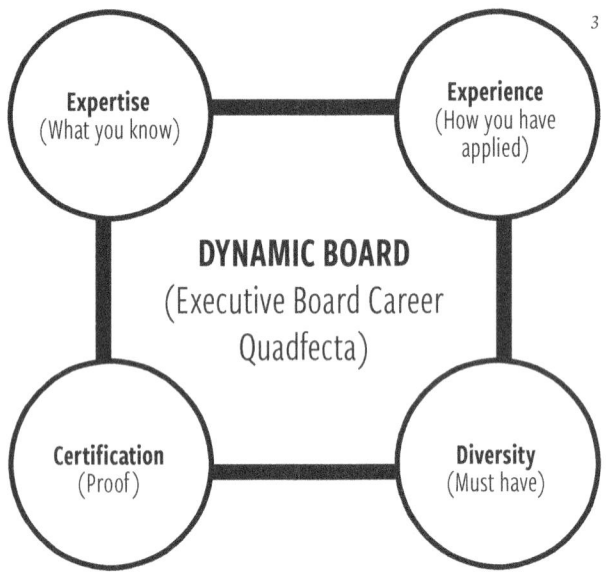

3 Adapted from 'Across The Board - The Modern Architecture Behind an Effective Board of Directors,' Mark A. Pfister © March 2018 - Chapter 13: 'Board Member Evaluation & Selection' pgs. 164 - 165.

These four quadrants of expertise, experience, certification,[3] and diversity are inclusive of all the areas that align qualified board members with CEOs and their organization's structure and objectives. The combination of these four factors has helped us to place numerous people on boards, or as advisors, and has made a significant difference to the organizations for which they work with.

Understanding the value of each of these four aspects of board preparedness will prepare you for future success. We are going to cover each of these areas, starting with expertise.

EXPERTISE IS ESSENTIAL

If someone were to ask you which was more important, expertise or experience, what would you say? There may be some people who even conflate these two definitions. Experience has to do with the numbers of years you are doing something. If you worked at a job for twenty years you would have a lot of experience. However, that would not necessarily make you an expert. What if you'd never done anything to increase your knowledge and to know the system inside and out? An expert is someone who would take those extra steps and use them to improve their organization. This is why expertise matters. It offers proven results as an achievement.

> **An expert has proven success in their field and is a stand-out game changer.**

Being a forward moving game changer is the aspiration of any expert. They understand they gain their status through experience and a commitment to achieving more. These accomplishments are not just spoken results but ones that can be proven through data and numbers.

As someone hoping to earn your place on a board, your expertise will help you stand out. If you were at a company for five years and were able to massively improve their operations in some way, such as their technological efficiencies, and it made that organization more profitable you would have proven expertise. Consider this over someone who has worked there for fifteen years but has not pioneered or initiated any type of change at all. Who would you give the edge to? The expert, of course! Experts bring:

- Ideas and strategies to back them up
- Insights
- Accomplishments

With expertise, you also show that you have excelled yourself to a higher level. You are ready to be a teacher. This is beneficial because there will always be people who want to or need to learn. Teaching has already had an impact on Boardsi. We have brought on a highly experienced trainer, renown in his field, to start an educational program for us. These have already become quite successful for us. In 2021 we will be adding video courses for executives to take their board education to the next level.

What this teacher knows about architecting a board has delivered results that have improved Boardsi and our company vision and trajectory, as well as the organizations who bring on our trained board members or advisors. What makes this valuable information even more appealing is it teaches many of the same principles you'd learn in an elite MBA school without the same high level of cost.

This guy is absolutely "mind blowing," and I continue to learn things from him, even as CEO of Boardsi. How has he achieved this? I have seen him in action and know that he:

- Does his research
- Invests extensive time into his expertise
- Demonstrates successful behaviors
- Delivers proven results

All of us at Boardsi are fortunate to have him! Our gain is also our clients because they receive the wisdom of his vast and proven experiences in board building. Everyone wins with his presence in the organization, and this is how he demonstrates he is an expert. He is a stellar example of walking the walk.

Take this example. You are with a company for ten years and in your mind, you are making the right decisions and doing the right things. Still your company is not succeeding. Are you someone you would bring on to your board? Or would you expect more expertise and proven results? Proven results should be the aspiration. It is easy for a person to feel right and think they are doing what is right. However, you must determine what is effective. In this case, it is clearly demonstrated that time on the job does not necessarily equate to the results a company seeks. Expertise would have served them better.

The largest contributor to someone not developing expertise is their inability to stop feeling like they can control everything. A Jack of all trades is a master at none. This is the difference. The second largest contributor that would prevent a person from becoming an expert is their ego. Now, I am not going to get into the nuances of ego because that could be a separate book. Just know that most people know the status of their ego by:

- Their own acknowledgment
- A lack of career progression
- Not being able to claim expertise in an important area in their career

Avoid the ego and embrace a team. That will make a profound difference. You'll become effective and be honed on what makes you a valuable contributor to an organization. Remember, board members govern an entire organization. They had best know what they are doing!

> **Since board members govern an entire organization, including top executives, it is important that they have enough experience to make wise choices, but are also viewed as credible by others.**

This wisdom will serve you well.

Now with what I've shared so far you may feel that experience is not as important. However, it does have an important role to play for a board member.

EXPERIENCE SPEAKS

At Boardsi, our board candidates must have extensive and relevant leadership experience. This includes understanding the complex challenges of enterprise leadership. Leadership is the one skill that almost every company we have talked to says they need. Leadership stands out through using the experiences that have led you into leadership so you can be relevant, thereby meeting an organization's needs at a board or advisory level.

Leadership stands out because you are not coming into a company as a CEO who will be taking over operations. You're just leading the way with your experience and your expertise, which requires strong leadership. From the managers to c-suite executive, you need to place them on a path of success. Because of this, relevant sector experience matters.

> **An ideal board candidate has gained leadership experience in sectors directly relevant to the company's business or in professional discipline pertinent the company's key capability areas.**

This could include experience in one or more of the following areas:

Business
The board candidate is, or has been a CEO, COO, or other major operating or staff officer of a major public corporation. Successful outcomes have ensued, whether this was achieved through a private or public company.

Expertise Background
The areas of expertise that are most sought after and include the areas of marketing, finance, and business operations. These happen to be the key factors that are likely achieved through being a CEO, COO, CMO, or CFO.

Longevity
While there is no specific amount of time required for a CEO to be at their job before being considered for a board position at another business, five years seems to be a good average because it provides enough time to get to know the workings of an organization well.

Regulatory and Public Service
Experience working in a highly regulated industry, such as pharmaceutical, healthcare, or insurance, brings skills and experiences that are beneficial. Also, academic and nonprofit experience can provide valuable insights that a board and business benefit from.

Information Technology
Not everyone may agree with me, but I feel it's impossible to have an effective board member if they are not tech savvy. Technology plays a role in all businesses today.

International Experience
As businesses grow it becomes essential to bring international experience to the table. Having someone who can lead in this from

the get-go or shortly after a company has taken off will matter to any growth strategy.

Logistics

Understanding the ins and outs of product distribution, both national and foreign, is important for any business with physical goods as a part of their business model. Businesses win when they find an executive with experience that can take leadership and the strategy and put all the logistics together.

With experience in some of these important areas, a board candidate is well-equipped to show their leadership and better help other people that are running companies do the same thing.

Whatever the company is seeking, you want to make sure candidates are industry specific. On occasion we have placed candidates that are not industry specific to what that company was doing, but these candidates were also industry complimentary. These have been quite rewarding endeavors, ones in which the candidate and company are better for it. There is no doubt that experience matters, or certification, which is the third part of the quadrant.

CERTIFIED FOR THE JOB

Certification is just as important as expertise and experience. Through this step, it shows a board member's desire to be at their personal best. It provides "proof of know-how," which helps offer reassurance to a CEO and their organization before bringing on this board member.

Oh, it's more education. Did you just think this? You would not be alone. You may also be thinking this: *I'm getting older. I am a successful, experienced executive and I have expertise in this field. Why do I need certification?* One way to prove you are qualified is through certification. I know that many executives have lists of accolades that can be found on Google. You can see where they have been, what they have done. The proof is there. The difference certification will make is to the company you are perhaps joining. It says a lot about the business who is seeking out a candidate and the seriousness of their search.

> **Certification shows an organization that the person applying for the board is dedicated to being the best member they can be.**

The certification process also shows that a board position is important to the potential member. They have taken classes and courses to receive it. Plus, after a certain number of years (however long the certification is good for) they want to maintain what they've achieved and will get recertified, gaining further knowledge on what may have changed over the time since their last certification. Let's face it, things change quicker today than they ever have at any prior time in history. In the last few years this is more evident than ever before, especially when it relates to topics such as governance.

Governance changes within the laws all the time. It is the obligation of a board member with this expertise to stay apprised of this. Look at this statement that is put out there by the SEC: "SEC rules and exchange listings standards impose certain requirements on the pay structure of a public company." In general, these requirements rely on audit compensation and nominating corporate governance. Listing standards also allow for independent oversight of director nominations in lieu of a specific nominating committee. Each of these committees must have a charter that includes their responsibilities and authority prescribed by SEC rules. A board member that can serve best will understand that being certified can help keep up with these constant shifts in policy, guidelines, and law.

Marketing is another area that is continually shifting. I look back at how the mainstream marketing was all about magazines, but now it has a massive focus on social media. Understanding this will matter to an organization that has to effectively promote themselves or their product or service.

The Boardsi organization is certainly not the only business that will offer these types of certifications. They can be taken other places too (albeit at a more costly price tag most times). You could go to a place such as ACCD (American College of Corporate Directors) or a business school for an Executive Education program. It is equally important to note that many advisors are also taking these courses, although it is not a requirement for them. They still understand the importance of it.

Highly specialized top management training board members benefit from certification. It helps these individuals ensure their contributions to a Board of Directors is maximized. This happens through better targeting of your activities and relationship management with stakeholders.

These certifications are especially important, particularly if you plan on going international. You need to know the workings of every specific region, as well as overall.

Recently, I had a conversation with a venture capitalist (VC) who was looking at funding their first overseas venture for a client. They had so many questions. How does the stock work? Is it different for international than US based? These are just a few of them. It was a complicated process, and the VC came to us for details on how it may work and other things they would need to be aware of. We offered that experience to them.

Through certification you also learn about:

- Effective structure
- Processes
- Skills

- Tools
- Frameworks
- How to drive a positive board culture

These are some benefits that certification brings so companies know their board members are prepared to face challenges that may arise. You can be the board member who makes the difference. You can be the standout!

DIVERSITY UNITES

It may seem counterintuitive but the more diverse you can make a board, typically the better it will perform its duties. To start, we must identify the most common trigger words we think of and respond to when we hear the word diversity. I'm referring to:

- Sex
- Race

Yes, diversity between the sexes and race is important to a board because it offers great value, when combined with experience, expertise, and certification. The great news is that it is accessible to any CEO or c-suite executive who seeks to accept the challenge of learning and mastering an aspect of business. From there, helping organizations via a board position is a great next step to take.

The first thing you need to look at to find the right diversity formula for your board is the company. In specific, its values, mission, and vision. No potential member, whether a big name or not well known, is going to be effective if they are not in agreement on a company's values, mission, and vision. This takes place by not focusing on pictures and well-known names; it is done by judging the actions of the candidate to find their experience and expertise. Taking this step has led to more diversity than you might believe.

Definitely more than what would feel evident if you looked at a board of 60+ year old white men, alone.

You don't have to look much further than me to see how diversity comes from experiences, not physical appearances alone. You cannot judge a book by its cover. I consider myself diversified, despite being a big younger than the typical 65-year-old man. It's what I look like from the inside that sets me apart. Take a deeper dive into my experiences, both where I come from and the journey I've taken, and there is more to the story. This is the point: We all need to find out "the rest of the story," to borrow commentator Paul Harvey's iconic saying.

People are beautifully complex and diverse, naturally.

- We come from different regions and cities
- We have various financial statuses (from upbringing to current status)
- We have diverse educations, ranging from suitcase colleges (like me) to ivy league educations
- We maybe had to work to pay our way through college
- We are entrepreneurs
- We have experienced successes and failures

Each of us can bring something totally different to the table. It's great to have people of all backgrounds and experiences a part of a board. It is what builds the robust nature of it and brings out the best in the people who craft policy and decision for an entire company. Women add a valuable dimension to this.

If you were to take a look at the basics of a marriage and how a husband and wife are different, and bring different ideas, you can gain a better understanding. Not to be a marriage counselor but looking at a married couple that come together to see what they provide. If they have the values, mission, and vision defined and laid out for both short-term and long-term goals, and generally agree on those points, it will be a marriage that lasts a long time and grows green and blossoms.

A good marriage will have arguments but if you sit back, re-evaluate the values, vision, and mission, then you will see where your partner is coming from and adjust where needed to make your "garden" grow. There is no need to look at your neighbors' grass and think that it is greener than yours—just take care of your grass if you need to!

Diversity makes the marriage grow and blossom just like it can in a company! These are two different people who still come together with their thoughts and ideas. Transfer this understanding to a board and you learn that these members should strive for a similar thing. It is, without a doubt, our differences that make us stronger. If I bring an idea to a board meeting and the Harvard student tells me I'm wrong, it is going to spark a discussion. And then next thing you know, out of the discussion, you have a blend of an idea—an idea that is potentially the next game winner.

Another important point to consider is the effectiveness of the board for the long term. A group of 60-something males from the same background may be able to solve some problems but can they understand a variety of problems with expert-level experience? No, they cannot!

One must ask themselves, *if I have five sixty-year-old male board members with same background, what will they bring to the table?* That's different. This is where the true answer to effectiveness shouts "no" to us. Diversity will make a Board of Advisors/Directors a lot more effective. Having board members ranging in age, race, sex, where they come from, and how they got to be where they are today is appealing and necessary. Bringing a wide range of ideas to the table is also a part of the board's task. How else, if not through diversity, do you get an expansive range of ideas?

Point of notice: More states require a diversified board than ever before. I feel it should be a company mandate, with or without government regulation.

Once you come up with the idea of what the purpose your board and/or advisors will fulfill, then you simply seek the best of the best, not looking at race or sex, but simply skills, experience, expertise, and if needed, certification. With this approach, you can gain diversity while not losing sight of a company's vision, mission, and values. There is no more cookie cutter idea of what a board's makeup looks like.

Companies are showing the need for diversity and it's one of the areas Boardsi is quite helpful in. We do have a lot of companies coming to us with direct requests. One example is a pharmaceutical company that came to us and shared their requirements. Two female board members, that was their request. Moving past being female, these women also had to offer a resume with an area of expertise. Being a matchmaker to connect qualified board people with businesses that need them is one of our most important undertakings at Boardsi.

I do get that it is not always as simple as desire for making the magical connection. A lot of times people want to bring someone on to their board, but they are a male who does not fit within diversity criteria. Yet, they are phenomenal and would be a great asset. What do you do in this situation? All I can suggest is creating another seat if it is possible.

Most boards have ten seats on them; however, there is no limit.

Where there is room for someone with a unique skillset on a board there is most always room for that one more person. Fantastic experience and diversity are both realistic expectations.

GENERATIONAL DIVERSITY

How about generation diversity? Does your company have different generational board members? Most likely you do for your employees, and this should be the same for your board members. Different generations bring different ideas, different skills. Let's look at the primary generations today:

- Gen Z, Igen, or Centennials: Born 1996 to TBD
- Millennials or Gen Y: Born 1977 – 1995
- Generation X: Born 1965 – 1976
- Baby Boomers: Born 1946 – 1964
- Traditionalist or Silent Generation: Born 1945 and before

The Center for Generational Kinetics is an authority on the subject of all things generational. According to their website (genhq.com), "Generation birth years vary by geography, and you'll see varying characteristics in different parts of the world. The big events that affect a generation can be dramatically different across the globe or at least regionalized or national in scope, and trends can hit at different times.

"For example, being a Millennial in Athens, Greece, with its current unemployment situation, can lead to different expectations and behaviors than being a Millennial in Austin, Texas at the exact same time, where the job market is fantastic."

Have you ever wondered why people talk about Millennials so much? Here is a thought... Baby boomers have the parenting philosophy of wanting things easier for their kids. The impact of this is that we have now created millennials with a sense of entitlement. This is relevant because millennials are, as of this writing, the largest generation in the US workforce, and it will remain this way for quite a long time. In addition to this, they are the fastest growing generation of customers in the marketplace.

Millennials are known for bringing a different attitude when it comes to:

- Employment
- Sales
- Marketing

Yes, millennials play a significant role in our world and workplaces. So, do you have at least one Millennial on your board? You should. Perhaps a millennial is what can bring a fresh idea or shine some light on why your marketing is not working, why is the biggest generation not buying your product? As all this unfolds, Gen Z is growing and getting to the age of employment. They are consumers too. Are you ready for the age of influencers and trendsetters? You need to evaluate this in the short- and long-term to see how it will affect your business.

An important point of distinction is to understand how COVID-19 has affected these age groups financially. How will they move forward, especially Gen Z, who are just graduating college and walking into an entirely different world. In the US, it is a world that includes receiving free money and some not paying rent. You have to think what long term effects of this might be.

In all, you need to make sure that board members understand your service or product and how it reaches each generation. Learn about the generations and how will they react to what your company offers. Be aware! The Silent Generation has experienced WWII, the Baby Boomers experienced space exploration, Generation X saw the end of the cold war and the rise of mass media, and we can't forget MTV. Millennials (Generation Y) experienced the rise of the information age, internet, war on terror, Iraq war, and 2008 real estate downfall. Now Gen Z is participating in the rose of information, and has been around for the dot.com bubble, digital globalization, the social media boom, and, of course, COVID-19. These events all matter to your board and its ability to function in today's world.

THE TINYBEANS CASE STUDY

The Tinybeans case study offers an excellent example of how we can help companies prepare themselves for success and growth with technology-based products.

About Tinybeans
Tinybeans was founded in Sydney, Australia in 2012 by Stephen O'Young. The company created a picture sharing application that helps parents capture and organize their children's lives using photos, videos, and written messages.

The app has privacy features that allow parents to retain legal ownership of their content, unlike other social media platforms and employs a premium subscription and advertising model. According to Tinybeans, their app has 4.65 million users spanning more than 200 countries. The company's revenue is predominantly generated in the United States and Australia. The United States makes up 92% of the company's revenue, while Australia contributes to the remainder.

Overview
Tinybeans partnered with Boardsi to help recruit non-executive directors. Tinybeans was searching for experienced executives to help increase their footprint in the market. Six months into the recruitment process, Tinybeans hired Boardsi recruit, Kathy Mayor, to join their Board of Director's team.

Results
Tinybeans shares rose by 15.97% as the company announced the hire of a Boardsi executive member. According to MSN

(https://www.msn.com/en-au/money/markets/why-the-tinybeans-asxtny-share-price-is-jumping-16percent-today/ar-BB1asuqd):

"Family photo sharing app Tinybeans Group Ltd's (ASX: TNY) shares have risen by 15.87% so far in today's trading. At the time of writing, the Tinybeans share price is trading at $1.46 after closing yesterday's session at $1.26. Today's moves follow an announcement by the company this morning that it hired two new executives in its United States operations. The hires reinforce the importance to the company's business model of the US market, which is where 92% of its revenue comes from.

"According to the release, leading US executives, Andrea Cutright and Kathy Mayor, will join the company as non-executive directors commencing immediately. Both Ms. Cutright and Ms. Mayor have substantial experience in digital marketing – the exact skillset Tinybeans needs to increase its footprint in the market."

Testimonial

> "With Boardsi, the team reached out regarding a company interested in speaking about an independent non-executive board member role on the day that my resume was uploaded to the platform. I'm grateful to Boardsi for facilitating the introduction."
>
> Kathy Mayor
> Board Member
> Tinybeans

THE MATCHMAKER HIGHLIGHTS

As you now realize, there are four quadrants to consider when you first start seeking out a board candidate to start dating. These are:

- Expertise
- Experience
- Certification
- Diversity

Each of these concepts needs to be addressed. The pace and pulse of business today depends on doing this.

Here are questions and ideas to consider when you are looking for the best board candidates. Every time you need a new member, use this to help guide your decisions. You can keep this information in one place more easily if you use your Corporate Matchmaker journal for this. Don't be hesitant to put serious thought to paper on how you feel about these questions and ideas.

Expertise

- How much passion does the candidate have toward the company's values, vision, and mission?
- What need does the candidate fill?
- Can this candidate bring expert experience that does not conflict with their other obligations?

Experience

- What new ideas does this candidate bring?
- What value does the candidate's experience offer?
- How has the candidate's expertise increased with their experience?

Certification

- How will certification and recertification be beneficial to this candidate?

- What are the best certifications for this candidate to have for your company's board?
- Why does certification matter for this position?

Diversity

- What government mandated diversity quotas do I need to fill?
- What are sound strategies to bring in diverse candidates that have expertise, experience, and the right certifications?
- How does this candidate demonstrate diversity of background, thought, and governance?
- What generations am I not taking into consideration that I should be?

These questions in the four quadrants are imperative to great decision making. The Boardsi team focuses on bringing the people that meet your needs to your business and preparing those individuals who wish to become future board candidates.

Here are a few more questions that will matter in the process of matching a company to a board member:

- Does the candidate have the time to commit? (This is one of the first things you should vet.)
- How about flexibility of time? (It is hard to coordinate busy schedules but not impossible.)
- How focused on accomplishment is the potential board member? (Socializing is nice, even important, but it does not take precedence over the ultimate job of the board, which is to govern a company.)

All this information serves as an excellent foundational guide to take you into our next chapter's topic, which will cover the process that CEO's and their organizations go through in order to find the strongest, best qualified board members and advisors.

SEEKING MATCHMAKER TO FIND QUALIFIED CANDIDATES

We are entering an age where speed, flexibility, innovation, and execution matter much more than decades-old qualifications or antiquated experiences dressing up a lengthy resume.

GYAN NAGPAL

There are so many things to consider when finding the right candidates to build the best board possible for a business. The process involves the biggest first step: dating potential matches to see if they are a good fit for you, the company, and that your company is a good fit for them. This process is exciting, but it can be demanding. Like the quote above suggests, there is a lot to consider, especially since we live in an age where speed, flexibility, innovation, and execution matter greatly. Combine this with the need for diversity and challenges could arise.

I want to help you move past the challenges with practical insights that will make a difference in how you:

- Build the board that governs your business
- Seek out a board at a company you have an interest in and where you can fill a need

Knowing what is required of you and what you should expect in either situation will matter. Let's discuss each one in detail.

BUSINESS SEEKING BOARD MEMBER

Finding the best board member to meet a company's needs begins with three basic steps. These are:

1. A company calls Boardsi and expresses an interest in getting a board member for their organization
2. We collect information on the company to ensure we have the details necessary to present an overview on them that is appealing to potential matches
3. We determine which board members a company may need (not always who a company may feel they need)

I want to discuss what happens after a company expresses interest in finding a board member or advisor through Boardsi. This process is one that our entire organization has worked hard to finesse for our clients. Our goals are to be thorough, efficient, and ultimately, be the matchmaker.

If a company calls us to express a need for a board member, we already begin the search with an edge. We have already qualified potential members based on their experience and time of involvement. This is where testing prevails, as we are always preparing future board members through certification.

As for the company, we do research on the organization before we even take this first call. This step allows for maximum efficiency and productivity on our meeting. We will:

- Do a general Google search on the company and its CEO to gauge their credibility
- We do a PitchBook search on the company (this company offers insights on a business that exceed what you can find online)

Let me share a bit about why PitchBook brings high value to the search. They offer information that is unlike what you can find online for a public company, such as stocks and quarterly earnings reports. PitchBook has all that information and more. It's all organized neatly. They even have a high amount of information on private companies. If we need something and they do not have it, they have the expertise to gather information. At times, this includes possibly calling the company and interviewing some people to learn as much as possible.

With this information in hand before a call takes place, our business-to-business (B2B) team will be prepared for the telephone call, which lasts about an hour. During this call we cover:

- What a business wants to do
- What stages they are at

- If they are looking for funding
- Who the current board members and/or advisors are

As mentioned previously, the question of who is on your board often leads to a response in the way of a question. Why are people asking me this question? This tells us two things: 1) They have been shopping around for information, and 2) They are not understanding why this is important. This means our first task is to show them why the board is important to every goal and aspiration the business has.

Imagine if you were investing in a company and you were talking to John Doe. John tells you he has got this great idea but has no one to help him with it. If you had the funds, would you be glad to write John a check hoping he would put the deal he talked about together? Obviously, the answer is no.

However, if John Doe came to you and said he had everything, including a board of people who had expertise in the various areas that will help ensure his success, it would be a different story. If you're a venture capitalist, it would be much easier to fund this latter scenario, right? This also becomes an easier situation for these venture capitalists to commit to because they often have a board that understands these key elements and knows how to maximize their investments.

Once our onboarding call is complete, we have a "Q & A" with the potential client. This is something we email to them to respond to. The questions can be intense, depending on how much information we were able to obtain from PitchBook. We ask about:

- Funding
- Needs to fill (board member, etc.)
- Forms of compensation they will offer

Yes, some of this is repetitive but you need to be sure. Once this process begins, people's reputations are on the line. Everyone can get better results when we are thorough during this process.

Through all these steps we get a real sense of the kind of energy a company exudes. We are able to determine who the CEO and/or founder really are and what they are passionate about.

At this point, we have a good idea of what the company is about. This is essential to us finding them solid candidates to consider. Then we can send over a few possibilities that could be good matches and proceed from there.

The first goal we have at Boardsi is to present candidates that are a member of our organization to these companies. They have been vetted already and we have a thorough understanding of their qualifications. Additionally, these executives have already been through an onboarding call when joining our community.

FUTURE BOARD MEMBERS WANTED

The basic process is the same for bringing on executives to the Boardsi organization. This is the most common sequence of events:

- Person comes to our website to look at what we do
- Said person expresses an interest in being on a board
- A call is scheduled with us to find out about the community and the process, including how a private network gains them access to companies seeking board members

After this, if the interested executive decides to join Boardsi, we schedule an onboarding call for them. This call is especially important, because it is the start of us helping make sure we know this person's best qualities and offerings so we can match them up with a company that can use these skills. This is how winning situations are created.

During the onboarding call for individuals, this is covered:

- How to use the network
- Making sure they have time to dedicate to a board position
- The energy and style of the new member
- Gain an understanding of their skills
- Review LinkedIn and recommend updates, as necessary
- Get credentials and recommend ones that may be beneficial

Everyone understands the process and hopeful expectations better after this process.

One important thing to emphasize is patience. At times, we coordinate people and their board positions quickly. At other times, it can take a year or more.

We always find first group of candidates to present to businesses, these are ones that have demonstrated favorable skills with IQ, EQ, MQ, and AQ (yes, all those Qs do matter). They also have the skill sets, experience, expertise and sometimes specially if need the certification. However, at times these highly qualified people do not meet all the needs. Sometimes in a specific industry or specific skill set might be missing and when diversity is needed it can really narrow the search. That is when we go to the next group of qualified executives in our database, and it is usually focused on diversity. Or this could be the case for someone who needs a particular skill set, as well.

When this step is complete, we then reach out to those executives we feel are most highly qualified and give them an idea of what we are looking for. If the candidate is interested, we move forward with them. The connection is made. From there, depending on the CEO and their organization's comfort level, they can take over the hiring process or we can act as an intermediary with it.

Another benefit that Boardsi members receive is access to our platform. They can also search out businesses that are seeking board members and see if they are qualified. When doing this, we encourage the executives that are seeking a board position to also start to complete their board documents, as they will be required for any public company they join. We have the documents for this on our website and it is quite detailed.

YOUR DUE DILIGENCE IN THE PROCESS

There are many things that you can do as you prepare yourself to be ready to join a board. The companies will look for these things because they want to and because they must by law. This means that the more prepared you are to present them with outstanding information the better the outcome should be.

Creating Resumes and Board Documents
Putting together a strong resume or set of board documents is going to play a significant role in the process of joining a board. Let's begin with resumes. You need to understand this; resumes are always written from a management point of view. They say things like: I created a team. I did this... I grew a company from a million to a hundred million. Resumes are always hands-on and highlight the executive's involvement with it.

When you create a board document it is written from more of an advisory role position. You don't get all the credit for accomplishments. You do, however, become a part of the board that took a business from one worth a million to one valued at a hundred million. Board documents are written from a leadership point of view. In addition, questions are included regarding character and skillset. This document is guided toward showing you off as a board member, which is separate from showing you off as an individual.

With the board documents you will present your case as to:

- Why you have the right skills and qualities to join a company
- How your contributions can grow the company

With these documents in place and knowing we have screened executives to offer for consideration, the conversations can commence in good consciousness. When companies and executives are eager to engage in the process it becomes a fruitful process.

Engage in the Community

The private network at Boardsi is quite spectacular, I admit. It is an incredible resource for both executives and companies to meet. A person committed to this platform receives the opportunity to stand out. Why would you not want this for you or your company? It is particularly important if you are the CEO of a private company, compared to a major one, such as a hotel chain, for example.

The conversations could play out any number of ways. Here is an example of what we have seen:

A top tier executive comes to us and the business development team gets to know this person quite well. They begin talking with a company and as they learn about this human asset they begin to think, *oh my God, this executive would be perfect.* From there, introductions are made, and a relationship can develop.

From our perspective, we don't have our reps contact a company and put an offer out there right away for who we perceive to be ideal. We call the company up and see what their reaction would be to this person and share what we know about them—which is why us getting to know you is so important to our work. If the idea is appealing to the company, we proceed with introductions.

At Boardsi, it is also important for us to monitor executives who reach out directly to a company for an available position. This is also acceptable; however, we do like to ensure that the basic parameters are being met. For example, if a company says they need a female who has governance experience we would evaluate the effectiveness of a male who may not have certain certifications applying to that role.

Our ability to do this is a benefit to everyone. We do offer incredibly detailed descriptions of the needs our companies have. We start by delivering a description of the role and its criteria that is published. Anyone can read this that is a member of the site. If they meet the basic criteria they can click on the "next" button and go a bit deeper into the content.

This is where you can take a look at the executive that applied to the opportunity. During this step, we are obviously looking for a potential matchup. We take a deep look at the individual's skills and what industry they come from. Some opportunities are extremely specific and don't provide room for leeway. For example, an executive with a pharmaceutical background that is female. It is easy to verify this. Does this person have a background in pharmaceuticals? Are they female?

When someone does not meet the base criteria, we always reply nicely, stating what the company is looking for. An example of a reply is: This position is searching for diversity and they need a female board member.

> **If a candidate makes it to the stage of company review, we also mark that on the platform. People know what is going on and that is part of what makes us highly effective in our work at Boardsi.**

From there, people move through the process until they sit down with a company (or are passed on). The company has the choice at this point of communicating directly with the potential member or having us set up the initial call, if even just to offer an introduction. From this point, a conversation will take place.

Great Conversations

Most executives and CEOs have developed their ability to participate in an engaging conversation. The key is to make sure you are conversing about what's important from the perspective of a board member.

How to start a great conversation…for some it is easy and for others it takes a bit more work. Either way, it is important. When it comes to finding a company and a match on the executive side, we make the introduction and let it go from there.

Daniel Henry, one of the co-founders at Boardsi, has a lot of experience in this and here's how a great conversation has impacted his work.

Since we have learned about the needs of the business and the experience and expertise the executive can bring, we encourage the executive to focus on that. Learn the values, mission, and vision of the company to make sure they align.

Explain and focus on how you, as an executive, can bring your experience and expertise to the company and what difference it can make. Think of a few strategies and talk about those as well. Be excited about the opportunity and express your values. If it is a public company and you have certifications or are in a course, make sure you bring this up in the conversation.

Being where you are you know how to interview, just make sure you focus on leadership!

Networking

The word networking in this context does not apply to your use of the Boardsi platform. As an executive, it refers to the people you know. At times, that is just what a company may need in their board member—an individual who knows people, especially financers, and can make those introductions.

There is an intangible, yet valuable, benefit from people who:

- Know how to connect to other executives
- Build networks of trusted contacts
- Can make beneficial introductions

Are you this type of person? How can you see yourself contributing to an organization? These are questions you must ask of yourself as you explore and expand into possibly using your experiences to build a better board.

If someone is a board member and introduces you to five other executives, feeling that you may each have value for the other, that is powerful. It is through these introductions that fulfilling relationships are cultivated and harvested. Add in experience, expertise, certifications, and diversity, and networking takes on an entirely new, powerful meaning. To make this happen, there is no room for ego.

Ego
There are many acronyms for the word ego. Some of my favorites are "edging God out" like Felicia Pizzonia mentions in her book "Mind Candy" and "everyone's got an ego." It is true; we all are vulnerable to our ego, which is why we have to keep it in check. Not only for board positions but for growth and advancement in life. Lasting positive change is not rooted in an unhealthy ego. We need others and others need us; this is what can make life so rewarding at times.

There are some people who will apply to a board position because they feel they can grow any company. It's good to feel you can make a difference but bad to put your abilities ahead of what a company may specifically need. If they really need that female with pharmaceutical experience and you are a male without it, applying to that position is not the best use of your time.

I don't care how big of an ego someone has every industry remains different with unique needs. You must be mindful of this if you want to find your place at the table.

It is true that there are great crossovers that help bring people to a board that none of us would think were qualified at first glance. Not just assuming will help greatly in alleviating ego-based decisions.

Crossover Recruitment
Our work at Boardsi involves looking at all angles. At times, if we feel it could be a good fit, we will suggest somebody that may seem like they are not a good fit at first glance. This is usually the person whose expertise, networking, or experience has universal appeal and effectiveness.

At times...

Our innovation gets turned down (and this is okay)

Our innovative idea is complimented and accepted (and this is fantastic)

We try our best to open up those ideas when we're talking to a company. But a lot of times, especially publicly traded companies, if their mind is set on something—particularly diversity—the answer is no.

LinkedIn
LinkedIn is at the pulse of business today. Everyone looks there and if you have no presence or a poor presence you will lose out on opportunities. It's that simple, which is why I am being that direct.

Here are a few tips that everyone who seeks a board or advisory position should take heed to regarding their LinkedIn profile.

1. Keep it current: as you gain experiences and expertise, add it to your profile.

2. Make sure you have a professional head shot of you on the site.
3. Have your education and certifications laid out descriptively and thoroughly.
4. Make sure your grammar and spelling are impeccable (don't be shy about hiring an editor to assist with this).

Taking these steps, along with suggestions we recommend as members of Boardsi, can make a difference in how effective the search for a board member goes for both companies seeking board members and executives seeking a board. Making sure your LinkedIn is up to speed is also a great step to take toward you demonstrating the patience that will be required of you.

PATIENCE FOR THE PROCESS

> **Learning patience can be a difficult experience, but once conquered you will find life is easier.**
> Catherine Pulsifer

Knowing something will take time requires that you demonstrate patience. This is seldom easy to do, right? We want what we want right away. It is common for those of us who are go-getters to want to move faster than we are able to at times. However, patience for the process is as noble as it is necessary.

When I was a teenager working at Jack in the Box, I got that job quickly. I applied one day, interviewed the next, and got hired the following day. Three days to my first job. Not too bad, that's what I was thinking.

Then life progressed and I found out that going from showing interest to being hired takes significantly longer than three days for jobs with significantly more responsibility. That taught me—and should remind all of us—that this is not the pace of opportunity as we build our careers. That takes much longer!

We don't, get to jump from "I'm just this working at this company to get some experience" to becoming a CEO six months later. Unless you start your own company, that is. The process to build up experience and expertise takes time.

I also worked at a mortgage company and was the marketing director. My friend Mark had owned the company at that time. I learned a lot in my position and was given extensive freedom to grow, explore, and develop beneficial skills. These skills helped me grow as a person, as well as help the company grow too. Basically, as long as I produced on the marketing side, he was happy and would leave me alone.

One day, one of his loan officers, a great salesperson, came into his office for a chat. I just happened to be there. The guy said, "Mark, I want to sit in your seat." Whoa! I thought, that is bold (quite the ego). Mark owned the business, but he also had a few partners, one being his brother. What was this guy getting at? He was hardly the next one in line for this position. Mark answered brilliantly: "You know what, if you think you can have my seat, you can leave my office and go start your own company. Cause that's the only way you're going to be in my space."

Within a few months, this guy did quit. He went to work somewhere else, not as the owner but as someone doing the same job at a different location. I have no idea what ever happened to him. He was not someone I chose to be a part of my networking circle.

If people want to find shortcuts, there are ideas out there to help you get to the position of CEO more quickly. What you need to do is determine why you want to be a CEO. Is it to benefit your life or benefit a business? The answer should be the latter, because CEOs do surrender a lot of things in order to effectively run their business. Sacrifice is required. However, it is necessary to realize that sacrifices can be made without surrendering personal happiness and joy. Knowing this helps you be better prepared mentally for eventually accepting a board position if you are in pursuit of one.

I tend to chuckle when an executive comes to me and expects to be placed on a board within two weeks. It just does not work that way. Time and patience are required. This is true whether it is a private or public company, as well.

You can be a difference maker of success or failure. Be thoughtful and patient, choose wisely.

Sometimes people are fortunate, and they are placed quickly. Their qualifications match the needs of an organization. In these cases, we can get these individuals in front a company quickly. The most common reason this takes place is that the onboarding person may ask us if we are still looking for a position for a certain company, and if we are, that company gets the applicants info right away. Even then, it usually takes three months from that time to go through the entire process. Again, time and patience are needed. I could tell you the endless reasons these qualities are necessary in life, personally and definitely professionally.

My job is not to attempt to control companies and their processes. Personally, I find it to be a better process to hire a board member when it does take a bit of time. Quick to hire, slow to fire. This expression serves as a great reminder of how to approach a merger of a CEO and a board member—cautiously and steadfastly.

From the executive side of the equation, I find that it is really important for the person to understand what to expect from their relationship with Boardsi. Even after they land on our platform and start to look through the different board positions, they need patience. If they say, "Oh, there's nothing here for me," I could tell them that they are right. Sometimes, we don't have the right company in yet and other times the expertise and skills of the executive are not needed for a board at that moment. This can happen and it is not due to lack of effort. We are constantly seeking out companies and executives to match them up with each other. Because of this we do know two things:

1. When a company comes to us, we look through the executives in our database.
2. When the executive comes to us, we look for companies within our database.

One of the most stellar examples of patience comes from a member of Boardsi. This person took over 14 months to place, so it was a while, but he allowed us to do what we did best—network for him. He remained patient and didn't complain. One day he sent us an email, just following up on the process. His timing was perfect! We had just gotten off the phone with a business that seemed ideal for him. We replied and coordinated everything. He did get the board position with that company and has become a tremendous asset to them. This is a great reminder that it is not about making matches fast but making the right matches.

FANWIDE: A CASE STUDY

Great ideas and ways of implementing is the goal of many businesses today. FanWide offers a success story that comes at a perfect time, especially given new protocols due to COVID-19.

About FanWide
FanWide, founded in 2016, is a Seattle-based company that manages the world's largest bar network for U.S. and global sports organizations.

The company provides sports fan technology and AI for crowd safety, security, and guest experience. FanWide COMPL-AI ("comply") provides event health and crowd safety management software designed to help prevent coronavirus (COVID-19) spreading at public facilities and spaces. FanWide COMPL-AI uses existing security cameras and video management systems (VMS) with artificial intelligence (AI) computer vision to proactively detect and report compliance incidences. FanWide can customize every camera to capture capacity counts in specific areas, detect overcrowding, enforce face-mask compliance, measure temperatures, or run dozens of other safety, security, or guest experience AI Rules. The company can optimize business operations while increasing guest safety for a fraction of the cost of hiring additional staff.

Overview

FanWide partnered with Boardsi to find executives that had reach and experience in the hospitality and sports industries. Boardsi connected with executives in their vast sporting community network and interviewed multiple candidates. After a few rounds of interviews, Boardsi found an executive that had ties to Major League Baseball and was the perfect fit for FanWide.

Results

By finding the right executive connected to the MLB, FanWide is now able to reach their goal and is planning to break into the large sports market.

Testimonial

> *"FanWide was seeking sports executives to join our advisory board but found it hard to navigate this industry. Boardsi was a great partner and connected us with multiple executives with experience in the NFL, NBA, NHL, and MLB. Boardsi has a great network, it is worth a conversation to see how they can help you!"*
>
> *Symon Perriman*
> *CEO*
> *FanWide*

THE MATCHMAKER HIGHLIGHTS

People are looking at you now. Each step you take forward will matter.

You've learned about what the process looks like as you seek out a board to join. If you are a company CEO you have learned a bit more about what to expect from a board member.

The pursuit of connecting executives to boards where they can serve in positions of value is not one that happens fast. The process requires patience and the time you have is excellent for making sure you are as prepared as possible, both through self-evaluation and actual steps that can be taken to finesse your LinkedIn and other relevant documents that will be required.

Use your Corporate Matchmaker Journal and put some effort into evaluating your steps you need to take for success. Reflect on your personal attributes and areas where you feel you would benefit from improvement. These questions will guide you. You can either answer them or use them as inspiration for different thoughts and ideas you have.

- I am an executive seeking a board. How can I best prepare for the process?
- Are there certifications I can earn?
- What strengths do I bring?
- Which board positions do I feel I would be strongest at?
- Is my LinkedIn profile professional and current?
- How is my relationship with patience?
- Does ego impact me in harmful ways?
    - Now?
    - In the past?
    - How have I grown from this?
- What crossover areas do I feel I would be qualified for?

- Am I comfortable with professional conversations focused on sharing value I offer to others?
    - Are there ways I can improve?
    - How?
- Do I have a solid network of people I trust?
    - If unsure, how can I build this network?
    - Do I feel this network is just for me or for others to benefit from, as well?
- How would I describe my level of patience?
    - What ways could I improve upon this and use this time more effectively?

These questions will really make a difference when they are followed up with solutions and actions that put them into motion. They will also be beneficial for when you hopefully receive an offer to join a board or advisory group. This is what we are discussing in the next chapter.

5

LET'S MAKE IT OFFICIAL

An effective group spirit on a board is one that attracts its members, makes them want to work with one another, and gives them a sense of pride and satisfaction in the program and the board itself.

CYRIL HOULE

This quote sounds like a dream come true. Can you imagine having board members working together in harmony, finding satisfaction in what they do and the results it delivers for the company they are a board member for? The idealistic description offered in the quote is easier to accomplish than you may have realized. I can say this with confidence because by the time you get to this point, you are working with a candidate or candidates that are passionately aligned with the set values, vision, and mission of an organization.

The processes for how you come to terms with individuals, to either join a board or become an advisor, are important. Also, how to proceed with each type of position is different, which is why I will cover each one separately, starting with bringing somebody on to serve as an advisor for your organization.

BRINGING AN ADVISOR INTO YOUR ORGANIZATION

Companies set up their various boards differently today than they have in days past. Most notably, this includes having a Corporate Advisory Board (or Board of Advisors). This is a trend that is not industry specific or product specific. It literally spans across all companies in all industries, including companies that are large and small, public or private, and with different entity statuses. There is obviously a good reason for doing this and that is the one major distinction between what a board member contributes, and the risks involved, compared to someone who serves as an advisor. That reason has to do with fiduciary responsibilities.

> **Advisors are not elected and have no authority to make any business decisions. This means they do not owe any fiduciary duties to the shareholders of the company by virtue of their advisory role.**

Not having fiduciary responsibilities for your advisor recommendations is appealing for obvious reasons, accountability being the one with the bright spotlight on it. Compare this to a board member who has fiduciary duties and is subject to liability arising from any breach of those duties.

For a company, using advisors is a great strategy that can lead to fantastic benefits, overall. An advisor contributes to the company's management and strategic planning without the duties or the liability exposure of a director. However, there are certain elements that need to be in place in order to keep everyone on the same page and cover all the legalese.

For starters, as a matter of practicality and legality, a company should define its relationship with advisory board members in a written agreement or perhaps a policy. I personally feel that a written agreement for every advisor is the best decision you can make as a CEO. It does not have to be a standard agreement; there is flexibility. This is important because you will bring on various types of advisors for different reasons. This means that each advisor could have a different structure.

Please note: There is no legal requirement to have any particular documents for an advisor, however, having them is a smart move. Laying out expectations helps to avoid misunderstanding, confusion about the role, and also works to protect the company's interests by limiting the liability exposure.

Occasionally you will find that a business has a consulting agreement with someone. In this context, I strongly feel that becoming a member of the Board of Advisors should be viewed as the next level from a consultant. Consultants are usually paid by the hour; advisors receive compensation in many forms (which will be discussed further into this chapter). So, if you are just looking to solve a problem, get a consultant and solve it. Compare this to an advisor and the expectations you may hold: These are people you want to be around a long time and want to develop a relationship with the company. Perhaps they are even future board members!

CONSIDERATIONS TO DOCUMENT

Whether a company uses a formal agreement or an onboarding memo that outlines the role of a particular advisor and/or the advisory board, specific information should be detailed in the document. This will protect both personal and company interests.

Document all these considerations in a written format.

- A description of what is expected from the advisor. This lists out specific duties and functions to be performed.
- Discuss compensation. Whether it is monetary or equity, it should be clearly defined and laid out.
- Specific duties need to be defined.
- The level of confidentiality that is required.
- Terms of service should be included. An advisor can quit at any time and an organization can terminate the relationship at any time, as well.
- Participation rights conflicts should be addressed. This is what will ensure that no other agreements that an advisor has entered into conflict with their role for your organization.
- Protection of intellectual property must be addressed. This is imperative because theft of intellectual property is a major concern in businesses today.
- Any possible conflicts of interest need to be addressed. For example, if you are working with a software system for one business you should not do the same for another similar type of business.

Whatever agreement is made, the company's board should formally approve the creation of the advisor relationship or advisory board, along with a resolution or a written consent, including adoption of an Advisory Board Agreement.

You will also need to address other details to keep the advisor and company on the same page. These include:

- Note who the advisor will report to: This could be a board member, the CEO, or another executive.
- Who services will be provided for: This could be to board members or directly to management.
- Authority to act: An advisor cannot act as a representative for the company or take actions that imply this individual has this type of authority.
- Duties specific to company: This includes the number of meetings, conference calls, or other events that an advisor must attend, as well as all preparation for such meetings. This would also include other duties that a company and advisor have agreed upon such as identifying business opportunities or assisting the board with management communications.
- Overall expectations: The advisor is aware of all expectations and serves based upon what he has agreed to while understanding that this person is serving at the will of the board.

Note: If the company is private a lot of times the Board of Directors is made up of partners. For advisors, this means they will work directly with management/Board of Directors because they are one in the same.

THE TERMS OF SERVICE

Knowing an advisor serves at the will of the board is an important aspect of their role. It serves two purposes:

1. It gets advisors on the same page as the board or CEO regarding the minimum commitment expected.

2. The company receives a graceful exit to the relationship if it does not meet their needs.

I want to discuss the second choice regarding the terms of service. The one thing an advisor must do—without exception—is add value to the organization they are serving. If the relationship heads in the wrong direction it is considerably easier to terminate someone who is not adding value.

Let's say a retired guy becomes an advisor. Six months pass by and then he decides to re-enter the workforce full time. Suddenly, he does not have time to serve in an advisory capacity. He cannot make it in to do anything he'd offered to do for the company as an advisor. He may decide he should leave the position, or the company may decide he should. Either party can do this because there is no guarantee.

Situations such as this example are a reason why members for a Board of Advisors are on the rise. This flexibility to make changes to who contributes in this capacity serves a valuable purpose by providing flexibility for individuals serving in these positions. If someone serves on the Board of Directors, they are likely to have a one-year-plus term. If a person is only a few months into their board term and things change it creates chaos, while not offering an easy out.

COMPENSATION

There are different ways to compensate an advisor, dependent on the company and the work the advisor will be doing for them. Again, it is important to note the compensation that will be given in either the agreement or onboarding memo.

Compensation needs to address:

- If payments are received on an hourly, monthly, quarterly, etc. basis
- Which party is responsible for expenses
- How expenses must be recorded

When an advisor is compensated, the amounts and timing of payments should be specified. If the compensation involves an equity component, then there will be many more issues for consideration and much more documentation involved. I don't go into the vast details of that in this book. Just know that a lot of advisors are brought on with a mix of pay and equity.

You will also find times when an advisor takes pay only, no equity or the opposite—equity only, no pay. This type of flexibility probably seems maddening, but it is the result of finding terms for compensation that meet both the company's and advisor's needs.

COMPENSATION SCENARIO FOR MEMBER OF BOARD OF ADVISORS

Here is one scenario on how compensation could play out for an advisor.

If an advisor has been given the expectation to network for the purpose to bring investors to the table and maybe they invest in the business, as well, they would get a specific percentage of equity for a specific amount raised. This could be written into the agreement. By participating in company meetings, and offering ideas and driving company growth over time, you could receive a vested percent of equity over time. Might be 1% of the company and every year for the next three years, ending in up to 4% equity. This is assuming you are vested for four years with the company, bringing strategies to create growth since this was the expectation.

At the end of the agreed upon term of four years you could leave your advisory role with 4% equity in a company and walk away. Unless things are heading the right direction and there is an exit strategy, and you are still an added value board member, then you come to new terms or continue with terms as defined.

Or you could have a scenario where you earn 1% equity for every $100K you connect the company with. The options are endless and an opportunity for companies to get as legally creative as they desire to. It will depend on what the company is trying to accomplish.

> **Each advisor brings different skills, experience, and expertise to the table. This is why advisor agreements need to be customized for every person.**

It is natural that a company would expect different things from different advisors. Not everybody knows investors, so not everybody might have that clause in their participation, information. and participation rights. Not everyone has experience with M & A or marketing. Every advisor does do one thing: They play their role with the goal of growing the company while keeping the values, mission, and vision in focus.

NOTIFICATIONS

Notifications have to do with communication, which is a major topic and the subject of the next chapter. When it comes to the topic of agreeing to terms, it is important for the company and their advisor(s) to agree what information will be provided to the advisor. (By law, this is not a requirement. It lies at the sole discretion of the company.) This information may pertain to:

- Corporate books and records
- Notice of meetings of the Board of Directors
- Information provided specifically to the directors

I do feel that if you want a great advisor you will have to provide them with information so they can be effective in their role. Withholding information does not help an advisor "guide the ship."

Basically, in order to ensure that the advisors can assist the board or management effectively, the company should provide copies of all notices, meetings, and minutes from relevant meetings. Before any Board of Advisors meeting, they should have access to the agenda so they can go over it and bring up any input they have.

Gaining access to these things obviously follow strongly with the next topic that should be a part of the process of bringing on an advisor. It requires a high level of confidentiality, as any information an advisor receives from a company should be deemed as confidential and privileged. Ensuring that you exercise the utmost integrity is critical.

One other notification that should never be overlooked is disclosing possible conflicts of interest. Both legally and ethically, this must be done. Ideally, way before you get to the step of drafting this document this will be information already disclosed and evaluated. It can be rather tricky if such information doesn't come out until this stage.

If you brought on an advisor, one who is also a CEO in a similar industry, that can be great. However, if they are a competitor, no matter how valuable you may view their insights it is not a great idea to sign up for such a direct conflict of interests. On the slight chance that you do have an advisor who also has a conflict, I recommend disclosing it and setting up parameters of what is acceptable and what is not. Both parties being aware of it is the primary concern.

For the record, this usually is not a problem because if there is a direct conflict, their employer they work for will not allow them to keep their job and advise the competition. This makes perfect sense. This is also the reason why our Boardsi team tries to check this out at the beginning of a process; it saves a lot of time and energy for us and it looks better than if we didn't bring this up when we could have and saved an unpleasant situation from progressing.

Overall, the more advisors and companies are in "the know" and notified of potential problematic areas the stronger the relationship will be. I am a strong advocate of taking all these measures because they lead to better business.

INTELLECTUAL PROPERTY

It seems strange for me to even have to say it, yet I am going to. Protecting intellectual property is super important. A company should take steps to protect assets that are created for the benefit of their organization.

When an advisor creates something for a business, steps must be taken to ensure the intellectual property stays with the business. This is why the agreement should contain an expressed assignment to the company for any development or work created by the advisor within the scope of his or her engagement. When doing this, also document the use of the company's confidentiality or proprietary information.

ONE LAST THOUGHT...

Your Board of Advisors serves as an excellent resource for future board members. A person can move from an advisory position to a Board of Directors position, having shown value to the company and being a fierce advocate for its value, mission, and vision.

The great relationships that individuals develop and build in these situations has proven to be beneficial to companies and their cultures. The biggest setback you may have in this situation is if someone prefers to keep advising rather than taking on the fiduciary responsibilities that come with being a part of the board. If it is not broke, why fix it?

Think of a company owner's point of view, as well. It's like a wine tasting. You are not going to buy a bottle of wine just because someone tells you that it is a great bottle of wine. Everyone's taste buds are totally different, so it is good to get a sample of it. Once you figure out which wine is great for your palette, you can buy that bottle. In business, before you put somebody in the responsibility of being on your Board of Directors, it is easier to do if you've experienced success working with them as an advisor first.

I get it, there is a certain appeal to getting paid with fewer responsibilities. You can still contribute something. However, a board position is the next level and a stronger resume listing than that of an advisor.

WELCOME TO THE BOARD

The Board of Directors is the governing body of a company. Therefore, it comes with a lot more responsibilities than what advisors are a part of. To begin with, its directors are normally elected by the subscribers, shareholders, or stakeholders of the firm, generally at an annual general meeting. Their every action and decision are based on having the ultimate authority and it is done with the intent of serving the subscribers' or shareholders' interests in a company.

These board tasks include:

1. Setting a company's policies, objectives, and overall direction
2. Adapt bylaws
3. Name members of the advisory, executive, finance, and other committees
4. Hire, monitor, evaluate, and fire the managing director and senior executives

5. Determine and pay on dividends
6. Issue additional shares

Clearly, the responsibilities are more immense. In addition, all its members might not be engaged in a company's day-to-day operations. Despite this, the entire board is held liable under the doctrine of collective responsibility for the consequences of the first policies, actions, and failures to act.

The members of a board usually include the senior executives, which are called inside directors or executive directors. The board also includes experts or respected persons chosen from the wider community. These people are called outside directors or non-executive directors. Together, they make up the board's composition.

When you are on a Board of Directors you even have to carry insurance for the position; not paid for by the company but by the person on the board. This is called Directors & Officers Insurance. This insurance is necessary because if they guide the company in the wrong direction, they can be held liable. If they were the one in the lighthouse guiding a ship and it crashed into a rock, they would hold the responsibility.

LET'S TALK TERM LIMITS

A person who serves on a board will also be subject to term limits. This helps the board member to avoid burnout, for one, and for two, it also enables the board to adjust its leadership to suit changing organizational needs. These actions help to protect the board and chief executive from an ineffective chair.

Earlier I mentioned how people's lives change and things happen, constantly. By having annual meetings and a rotating schedule for bringing on new board members you can more easily change the makeup of the board. For example, if you had a board of all males in their mid-sixties, and they were fixed for ten years, that could leave a detrimental gap in the company's best interests. They might not do anything of value, only show up and get paid. And suddenly, five years into that ten-year span, a law comes out that says you need to have diversity. What do you do? You're stuck for five more years with a very non-diverse board. You would have to get this group to approve adding a diverse board member on. Do you think that candidate would represent the true value of diversity? Likely not. This is why terms are one-to-two years at most, especially if you are a board chair.

According to the website Leading with Intent, here are some of the most common board structures:

- A Chairman of the Board is two consecutive one-year terms
- Vice-chairs and other members can serve unlimited one-year terms
- 72% of nonprofit boards have a have term limits, with the most common board member term structured being two consecutive three-year terms

What is the reason for longer terms for vice-chairs and other board members? The answer: Some of these other positions require depth of knowledge, as well as institutional knowledge, and it just is not prudent to change who holds the position yearly. Take the position of Treasurer, for example. This person would be difficult to retrain and replace annually or even every other year. Finding these continual replacements could be tricky.

If nothing else, you should ponder the results of what could come to be if you kept the same board members serving for twenty or even thirty years. My personal opinion is that after ten years you are no longer adding value to the company. This sounds a bit harsh but consider this... If you look at our last twenty years, things have changed significantly in business and the way it is conducted—even what is expected. The further back you go, say to the 1940s, the more change you see. Fresh ideas and perspectives come with new blood during these changes; old blood can no longer meet these same essential needs a business will have.

Here is another example, you are on a Board of Directors for a publicly traded company, and you have been there for five years. Everything you do is out in the open (it's a public company) and for one or other reason the company experiences a "bad" quarter—you did not meet your goals. The shareholders are obviously not happy! In addition to this, all of a sudden there are two new companies in your industry that just went public, and they are thriving and growing; this is a young and energized company, and they are crashing your numbers.

How did this happen? That company has been the leader in that industry for so long, how did they not see this coming? Well, this happens all the time, companies enjoy being on top, thinking there is no competition. They get stagnant, the ideas are no longer flowing, energy is lower. Meanwhile, the new and upcoming competitors have been studying the giant and finding new ways to get better, and they did!

This is another reason why you need new board members and need to be innovative. So, to stay on top you need the best of the best. Some people look at a Board of Directors as top of the chain. That is true, they are making the decisions, but I also like to look at it as bottom up, I see them as the foundation of the company. That foundation is imperative to the company's success because it keeps them steadfast through any storm the company weathers. The way all this is gauged is meeting the quota…so meet the quota.

A CRITICAL NEED

With the amount of governance and legal framework of a board and all it does for the company it serves, it is important that we discuss legal counsel. It is necessary, whether this person serves on the board or is an advisor. Not having a lawyer at your disposal or general counsel for your company is a bad move.

Yes, they are expensive but not compared to what legal fees could be if something, God forbid, went wrong. If you work in a business that has a lot of legal dealings, you will definitely want the expertise of a lawyer at your disposal. How to best bring them on is something that your board can help determine.

FINANCIAL COMPENSATION

Board members are not paid an hourly rate. They receive a base retainer that averages around $25,000 per year. I know that seems low, but it is an average between small businesses and large ones.

On top of this annual fee, the board members may receive compensation for specific activities, such as:

- Attending board meetings
- Teleconferencing

Some companies may pay a higher rate and not compensate for extra meetings.

From my research, bigger companies surprisingly paid much more than the average. The median director pay in the US for our largest companies was around $250,000. That was back in 2015. Taken from corpgov.law.harvard.edu, these compensations have been standard:

- *Retainers and Meeting Fees.* In 2019, the average annual cash retainer for S&P 500 directors was $126,200. This reflects an increase of 18% over the previous five years—in 2014, the average was $107,383, in 2009, $75,893 and, in 2004, $49,727. Only 9% of S&P 500 companies paid directors for attending board meetings, and only 12% paid directors for attending committee meetings. However, some S&P 500 companies pay a meeting fee in lieu of a retainer and cap directors' aggregate meeting fee opportunity at a specified amount.

- *Equity Compensation.* 77% of S&P 500 boards grant directors equity in addition to cash retainers, representing a slight decrease from 10 years ago, when 79% of such boards granted stock. Additionally, 37% of S&P 500 boards granted stock options in 2009; whereas only 11% do today. Stock awards represent 57% of total average director compensation for S&P 500 companies, and option grants represent 3%.

This chart helps to solidify this point:

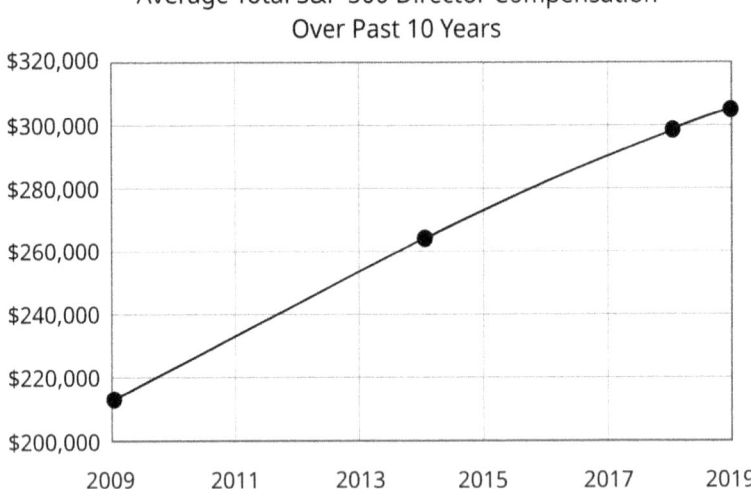

At other times, companies pay at least a portion to their members in stock options rather than cash. These are individuals who often hold two or three different positions at different companies, and they choose stock. It becomes a matter of what both parties can agree upon in the end.

NEGOTIATIONS

Negotiations often lead to a compromise. You know what they say about compromises: Both sides feel like they gave away too much.

At the end of the day after you've done all your homework on the person that is being considered for a board position, you should feel great about coming to terms with the person you have chosen to serve on the board. You know they agree with the "Big 3," which are the company's values, mission, and vision. All that is set is to move forward and reach an agreement.

I feel the best place to begin is to evaluate the goal you are looking to gain from this executive. Let's cover some of these goals.

The goal could be to tap into an executive's network. If this is the case you should know if the future board member is going to make an introduction and then pass the baton, or if they will be involved to a much further extent. The more they are involved the more of a factor that is for higher compensation.

This brings on the need to evaluate what happens with this new connection. Do they become an advisor, or how do they fit into the plan? One idea a company can do is to pay 1% equity for a board member who brings on a high value advisor to the organization.

Perhaps the board member can help with funding. In this case you could offer him or her another percent for every $100K of funding they connect the company to.

How long-term you envision having an advisor or board member be active with your company also needs to be considered. If they are meeting a short-term need that needs to be weighed against what you would offer to someone who can offer long-term value to the company.

All these factors change how you choose to negotiate, each offering a unique viewpoint. You must also be mindful that the hopeful board member is coming to the negotiation table with a number in mind. I think that most people who believe in the "Big

3" are going to be happy with something reasonable to begin with. This person can always work toward more by proving themselves, thereby ending up with a bigger position or pay at the end of the day. This is a great approach to take for start-up companies because they most likely won't have any monetary pay; they will have equity to offer though.

And last, I want to share a personal opinion with you of what should not be acceptable. That is "nothing." If a company says they want you on their board but until you serve them for a year and prove yourself, you will not earn anything. After a year, you may earn 1%. These are not good terms for somebody and thereby I do not recommend accepting them. No use in spinning your wheels.

A STORY OF "CONDITIONS"

One of our clients recently signed with a company. At first, they were offering a really small percent—it was almost a joke, really. This person countered right away. They shared what they had contributed already: They had shared some of their network and connected them with two potential investors. They had proven value!

This client countered and explained why they were doing so. The company did understand and actually felt a bit foolish in the end. A great agreement was reached.

The meaning behind this story is that at times companies do not know what is acceptable. They have never asked, so until it becomes a topic it remains unknown. It is not uncommon for company executives seeking out an advisor or board member to approach Boardsi and get our perspective on how to best negotiate this entire process. What is reasonable? The answer to this depends on the answer to this question: What is the goal?

WHAT THE CONTRACT LOOKS LIKE

This section contains two examples of agreements to help give you an idea of what they look like. Keep in mind: I am not a lawyer and I recommend you use one to complete your agreement.

Advisor Agreement sample: (https://www.foundersspace.com/wp-content/uploads/advisor_agreement.pdf)

* * *

Each such expenditure or cost shall be reimbursed only if: (i) with respect to costs in excess of $100, individually, Advisor receives prior approval from the Company's CEO or CFO or other executive for such expenditure or cost, and (ii) with respect to costs in less than $100, individually, provided Advisor furnishes to Company adequate records and other documents reasonably acceptable to Company evidencing such expenditure or cost.

4. PROPRIETARY INFORMATION; WORK PRODUCT; NON-DISCLOSURE.

a. Defined. Company has conceived, developed and owns, and continues to conceive and develop, certain property rights and information, including but not limited to its business plans and objectives, client and customer information, financial projections, marketing plans, marketing materials, logos, designs, technical data, inventions, processes, know-how, algorithms, formulae, franchises, databases, computer programs, computer software, user interfaces, source codes, object codes, architectures and structures, display screens, layouts, development tools and instructions, templates, and other trade secrets, intangible assets and industrial or proprietary property rights which may or may not be related directly or indirectly to Company's software business and all documentation, media or other tangible embodiment of or relating to any of the foregoing and all proprietary rights therein of Company (all of which are hereinafter referred to as the "Proprietary Information"). Although certain information may be generally known in the relevant industry, the fact that Company uses it may not be so known. In such instance, the knowledge that Company uses the information would comprise Proprietary Information. Furthermore, the fact that various fragments of information or data may be generally known in the relevant industry does not mean that the manner in which Company combines them, and the results obtained thereby, are known. In such instance, that would also comprise Proprietary Information.

b. General Restrictions on Use. Advisor agrees to hold all Proprietary Information in confidence and not to, directly or indirectly, disclose, use, copy, publish, summarize, or remove from Company's premises any Proprietary Information (or remove from the premises any other property of Company), except (i) during the consulting relationship to the extent authorized and necessary to carry out Advisor's responsibilities under this Agreement, and (ii) after termination of the consulting relationship, only as specifically authorized in writing by Company. Notwithstanding the foregoing, such restrictions shall not apply to: (x) information which Advisor can show was rightfully in Advisor's possession at the time of disclosure by Company; (y) information which Advisor can show was received from a third party who lawfully developed the information independently of Company or obtained such information from Company under conditions which did not require that it be held in confidence; or (z) information which, at the time of disclosure, is generally available to the public.

c. Ownership of Work Product. All Work Product shall be considered work(s) made by Advisor for hire for Company and shall belong exclusively to Company and its designees. If by operation of law, any of the Work Product, including all related intellectual property rights, is not owned in its entirety by Company automatically upon creation thereof, then Advisor agrees to assign, and hereby assigns, to Company and its designees the ownership of such Work Product, including all related intellectual property rights. "Work Product" shall mean any writings (including excel, power point, emails, etc.), programming, documentation, data compilations, reports, and any other media, materials, or other objects produced as a result of Advisor's work or delivered by Advisor in the course of performing that work.

d. Incidents and Further Assurances. Company may obtain and hold in its own name copyrights, registrations, and other protection that may be available in the Advisor. Advisor agrees to provide any assistance required to perfect such protection. Advisor agrees to take sure further actions and execute and deliver such further agreements and other instruments as Company may reasonably request to give effect to this Section 4.

e. Return of Proprietary Information. Upon termination of this Agreement, Advisor shall upon request by the Company promptly deliver to Company at Company's sole cost and expense, all drawings, blueprints, manuals, specification documents, documentation, source or object codes, tape discs and any other storage media, letters, notes, notebooks, reports, flowcharts, and all other materials in its possession or under its control relating to the Proprietary Information and/or Services, as well as all other property belonging to the Company which is then in Advisor's possession or under its control. Notwithstanding the foregoing, Advisor shall retain ownership of all works owned by Advisor prior to commencing work for Company hereunder, subject to Company's nonexclusive, perpetual, paid up right and license to use such works in connection with its use of the Services and any Work Product.

f. Remedies/Additional Confidentiality Agreements. Nothing in this Section 4 is intended to limit any remedy of Company under applicable state or federal law. At the request of Company, Advisor shall also execute Company's standard "Confidentiality Agreement" or similarly named agreement as such agreement is currently applied to and entered into by Company's most recent employees.

5. Non-Compete. During the Term, Advisor shall provide the Company with prior written notice if Consultant intends to provide any services, as an employee, consultant or otherwise, to any person, company or entity that competes directly with the Company, which written notice shall include the name of the competitor. During the period that is six (6) months after the termination of this Agreement, Advisor shall provide the Company with written notice any time that Advisor provides any services, as an employee, consultant or otherwise, to any person, company or entity that competes directly with the Company. Notwithstanding anything to the contrary contained herein, Company hereby consents to Consultant providing services, as an employee, consultant or otherwise, to the following companies.

6. MISCELLANEOUS.

a. Notices. All notices required under this Agreement shall be deemed to have been given or made for all purposes upon receipt of such written notice or communication. Notices to each party shall be sent to the address set forth below the party's signature on the signature page of this Agreement. Either party hereto may change the address to which such communications are to be directed by giving written notice to the other party hereto of such change in the manner provided above.

b. Entire Agreement. This Agreement and any documents attached hereto as exhibits constitute the entire agreement and understanding between the parties with respect to the subject matter herein and therein, and supersede and replace any and all prior agreements and understandings, whether oral or written with respect to such matters. The provisions of this Agreement may be waived, altered, amended, or replaced in whole or in part only upon the written consent of both parties to this Agreement.

c. Severability, Enforcement. If, for any reason, any provision of this Agreement shall be determined to be invalid or inoperative, the validity and effect of the other provisions herein shall not be affected thereby, provided that no such severability shall be effective if it causes a material detriment to any party.

d. Governing Law. The validity, interpretation, enforceability, and performance of this Agreement shall be governed by and construed in accordance with the laws of the State of California. Venue for any and all disputes arising out of this Agreement shall be the City of Berkeley, State of California.

e. Injunctive Relief. The parties agree that in the event of any breach or threatened breach of any of the covenants in Section 4, the damage or imminent damage to the value and the goodwill of Company's business will be irreparable and extremely difficult to estimate, making any remedy at law or in damages inadequate. Accordingly, the parties agree that Company shall be entitled to injunctive relief against Advisor in the event of any breach or threatened breach of any such provisions by Advisor, in addition to any other relief (including damages) available to Company under this Agreement or under applicable state or Federal law.

f. Publicity. The Company shall, with prior written approval by Advisor, have the right to use the name, biography and picture of Advisor on the Company's website, marketing and advertising materials.

IN WITNESS WHEREOF, each party hereto has duly executed this Agreement as of the Effective Date.

COMPANY ADVISORY BOARD MEMBER

Signature: Signature:
Name: Name:

* * *

EXHIBIT A TO ADVISORY BOARD AGREEMENT

Services.

As a member of the Advisory Board, you shall:

- Participate in monthly Advisory calls which will last no more than ____ hours
- Participate in annual full day retreat
- Be accessible to Company to provide guidance on business and technology strategy issues on an as-needed basis

Compensation.

The Company shall issue Advisor a non-qualified stock option to purchase XXXX shares ("Option Shares") of the Company's common stock at an exercise price equal to ten cents ($0.XX) per share (which is the current value of each share). The Option Shares shall vest as follows: provided this Agreement remains in effect, XXX shares shall vest immediately and the remaining X,XXX

Option Shares shall vest at the rate of XXX shares per month on the last day of each month over 12 consecutive months.

* * *

Board Member Contract: https://sehub.stanford.edu/sites/default/files/BoardMemberContract.pdf

BOARD MEMBER CONTRACT

I, _____, understand that as a member of the Board of Directors of _____, I have a legal and ethical responsibility to ensure that the organization does the best work possible in pursuit of its goals. I believe in the purpose and the mission of the organization, and I will act responsibly and prudently as its steward. As part of my responsibilities as a board member:

1. I will interpret the organization's work and values to the community, represent the organization, and act as a spokesperson.
2. In turn, I will interpret our constituencies' needs and values to the organization, speak out for their interests, and on their behalf, hold the organization accountable.
3. I will attend at least ___ percent of board meetings, committee meetings, and special events.
4. Each year, but no later than Thanksgiving of each year and without having to be asked, I will make a personal financial contribution at a level that is meaningful to me.
5. I will actively participate in one or more fundraising activities.
6. I will excuse myself from discussions and votes where I have a conflict of interest.
7. I will stay informed about what's going on in the organization. I will ask questions and request information. I will participate

in and take responsibility for making decisions on issues, policies, and other matters. I will not stay silent if I have questions or concerns.
8. While I am a member of this board, I will make every effort to vote in every public election.
9. I will work in good faith with staff and other board members as partners toward achievement of our goals.
10. If I don't fulfill these commitments to the organization, I will expect the board president to call me and discuss my responsibilities with me.

In turn, the organization will be responsible to me in the following ways:

1. I will be sent, without having to request them, quarterly financial reports and an update of organizational activities that allow me to meet the "prudent person" standards of the law. (The "prudent person rule," applied in many legal settings in slightly differing language, states that an individual must act with the same judgment and care as, in like circumstances, a prudent person would act.)
2. Opportunities will be offered to me to discuss with the executive director and the board president the organization's programs, goals, activities, and status; additionally, I can request such opportunities.
3. The organization will help me perform my duties by keeping me informed about issues in the industry and field in which we are working and by offering me opportunities for professional development as a board member.
4. Board members and staff will respond in a straightforward fashion to questions that I feel are necessary to carry out my fiscal, legal, and moral responsibilities to this organization. Board members and staff will work in good faith with me toward achievement of our goals.

5. If the organization does not fulfill its commitments to me, I can call on the board president and executive director to discuss the organization's responsibilities to me.

Signed: by _____, Board Member
Date _____
and by _____, Chair of the Board of Directors
Date _____

DIVERSYS CASE STUDY

The Diversys case study provides a wonderful example of how innovation is made better by a board with a dynamic vision.

About Diversys
Diversys is a Canadian based company that was created to build a world where technology is used to make recycling supply and recovery management transparent, efficient, and easy. Diversys provides a one-of-a-kind suite of software that supports the circular economy and resource recovery organizations that administer, oversee, and enforce recycling and EPR legislation frameworks around the world.

Overview
One of the main reasons Diversys wanted to partner with Boardsi was because of Boardsi's international reach. The first match Boardsi found for Diversys had ties to the recycling world, which led to a perfect match. Boardsi then searched for another executive who had connections with the European community. Boardsi was able to efficiently match executives due to their network filled with connections in different countries ranging in many different skill sets.

Results

Diversys has been able to increase their reach and is poised to break into the European market. By bringing in the right executives that have valuable connections it makes it easier for organizations to navigate business hurdles with ease.

Testimonial

> "Being based out of Toronto I wasn't sure how working with Boardsi while building my board of advisors would turn out. I took a chance and sure am glad I did! Their team went over our needs and started the search process immediately. Within a few weeks, I had some resumes and a few of them were great. Now after four months we finally signed a contract with our first executive and are moving into searching for number two, an executive that is EU centric. Overall, I am very happy with Boardsi and the search process. As I continue to build out our board advisors, we will continue to work with Boardsi. I highly recommend any company to connect with Boardsi and am sure they will find you the type of executive you are searching for."
>
> Roger Barlow
> CEO
> *Diversys*

THE MATCHMAKER HIGHLIGHTS

We have covered the thoughts and expectations that take place when you are coming to terms with a company to serve them as either an advisor or a board member. Each area of service has distinct differences, thereby different obligations from the people who will serve.

The questions for this area will be divided into three parts:

1. For CEOs
2. For future board members
3. For your personal growth
4. Using your Corporate Matchmaker Journal, contemplate these questions:

CEO

- What is the goal of the advisor or board member my company wishes to bring on?
- What is ideal in terms of compensation? (Not free!)
- What is realistic in terms of compensation?
- What benefits will this person bring to the company?
- Does this candidate truly align with the company's value, mission, and vision (The "Big 3")?

Future Board Members

- What areas of expertise can I offer a board as either a member or as an advisor?
- What is my goal for serving the board?
- What is just compensation for this?
- In what areas do I have flexibility? Why?
- What does my ideal negotiation process look like?

Personal Growth

- What are my strengths at negotiating?
- What areas could I use improvement in?
    - What resources can I tap into for these improvements?
- What is my ideal relationship with a board as a CEO?
    - How about as an advisor?

- How about as a member of the board?
- What can I do today to become more effective in my pursuits of corporate leadership?

These are important questions to consider. They are helpful for knowing your worth and negotiating on it, as well as giving yourself direction to be of the utmost service to companies that you work with.

In the next chapter we are going to discuss communication, which is the cornerstone of everything that you do in business, from whatever level you are involved in. The topic is much more expansive than simply listening and relaying information effectively.

THE ART OF COMMUNICATION

Good communication is just as stimulating as black coffee, and just as hard to sleep after.

ANNE MORROW LINDBERGH

Communication is the pulse that breathes life into all business. It should be stimulating because it is forward moving and exciting, just as the quote above infers.

As you sort through all the executives who may be qualified to serve on a company board, you will end up spending many hours, days, weeks, and even months on the process. Once the hiring is complete, why would you ever jeopardize it with lackluster or ineffective communication? That would never make sense, yet it can happen. Here's how it can be prevented.

In order to make sure you take full advantage of what you have built you need to ensure your communication plan is set. Always communicate about:

- Where you're at with a project or task
- Where you're going with these projects and tasks
- What needs to be done next

These basics are a great start, especially when you keep communication simple. You do this by avoiding discussing all things with communication and remaining on a single specific point.

With these expectations—necessities really—in mind, I am going to break down the massive topic of communication into small, actionable parts. You'll find that when all these parts are added together, they make the whole of a business better and stronger.

BE FORTHRIGHT AND DIRECT

CEOs are busy people. This can sometimes make working with a board feel like an unnecessary addition to an already busy schedule. Especially when the pressure is on and time-sensitive decisions must be made. In these cases, it can be tempting for a CEO to work around a board or water down the facts in hopes of getting things done quicker.

Completing what you must get done in a more time efficient manner seldom works out with this approach. It might if you are lucky; however, if you are diligent, you will avoid this messy habit and situation. In the end, this action of convenience could create more work for you, as well as more pain down the road when you have to revisit the situation or explain yourself further. In times where this shortcutting is a temptation, pause and ask yourself why you built the board in the first place?

Always be forthright with the board and resist that temptation to present an incomplete story, plan, strategy, or angle for whatever it is you're trying to accomplish. Ignoring complicated issues that a board would feel compelled to address erodes trust. Furthermore, it does not facilitate successful outcomes. Communication with the board must always be:

- Truthful
- Transparent
- Comprehensive
- To the point

CEOs sometimes make the mistake of assuming that board members know more than they do. Although they know a lot and have significant influence, they typically do not have an in-depth understanding of the day-to-day working of the company like a CEO does. They are managers, which means they are busy people with their own set of prescribed tasks. In addition, they may also have a day-to-day job at another business. Limited time is precious time, and this means that when someone chooses to sit on a company's board you should ensure they are doing what you need from them in order to best fill their role efficiently and effectively.

It seems obvious, but board members should enjoy their meetings, not dread them. The people you bring on are achievers who appreciate meaningful, productive, and enjoyable gatherings. Being organized and prepared will help you be most productive.

> **The most sure-fire way to create a dysfunctional relationship with your board is to not fully prepare information that is needed before an important decision is made.**

This is particularly relevant for those decisions that are time sensitive. No one likes to be surprised and no one wants to feel like they are being backed into a corner when important decisions need to be made. During these times, continuous communication with the board becomes especially important. Follow these tips:

- Include board members in discussions and leave time for questions and answers.
- Don't assume that because one board director understands a topic with great depth that the others do too.
- Remember, the CEO is the one ultimately responsible for ensuring that all directors are informed on key issues; even when they incorporate help from another executive to do this.
- Be transparent and share both the good news and the bad news. If the board learns bad news about the project before you tell them, then you have lost their confidence.

These steps are logical and effective. For those of you who serve on a board, the CEOs attention to communication details is something you are likely to appreciate. Everyone benefits from clear and precise communication.

BE PROACTIVE

Communication must be proactive. Take action! Before meetings, communicate with all board members who will attend. For example, if a pitch deck is needed or some kind of a presentation deck, send it in advance. This will benefit everyone because it creates another opportunity for feedback and input. By sending these items ahead of time, you could also get replies that you may wish to include during the meeting. Doing this shows you are prepared and acting in this manner is important to both you and your work.

You should never hold a board meeting when you do not know where your board stands on key issues in advance.

The only way to be certain of this is through a proactive approach. Ensuring these measures are in place will help you flush-out concerns and achieve alignment on the problems and challenges at hand.

Also, never reserve bad news for the actual board meeting. This is super important. Bringing bad news to board members attention promptly—which is always before a meeting in which it will be discussed—will allow the member time to digest the information and gain a better perspective on a possible solution. Meetings that involve board members coming in with knowledge of bad news are ones where everyone can get right to finding possible solutions.

Another benefit to airing everything out prior to a meeting is that if you're going to face a good "talking to" or blowback of some sort, it is better to have that happen in private rather than on center stage and where the results will be recorded in minutes. A lot of times, if it is a specific problem and you have an advisor that deals with that area, you will want to bring this up to the board member directly and possibly have a solution for the problem before the meeting even starts.

I learned at early age that it is easier for me to communicate one-on-one, as compared to a group meeting. Back in high school, I used to freeze when doing a presentation, then I would start, and my face would be bright red. I'm not like that anymore, but I have never forgotten.

When communicating a problem, one-on-one is always easier, especially with an advisor. Ask for honest feedback and possible ideas—you never know what will arise out of the situation. As an example, I know a company that was struggling with their marketing. They were going to present this problem to the board and the CEO had no solutions. Most likely, the board was not going to be happy. Since the CEO had a good relationship with a couple of the board members, he reached out on a one-on-one level and talked it out. He did receive some feedback and his efforts made coming to the meeting a better experience. He was able to offer new ideas, not one idea but several. This gave the board multiple solutions that may solve their problem.

It turns out, this CEOs FEAR (False Evidence Appearing Real) was just that. There was nothing to fear, the solution created new ideas and those ideas created new growth strategies for the company. Don't fear the bad news. Face it and communicate about it. Don't feel alone on the island of bad news, because there is no need to if you do not procrastinate and choose to face and solve your problems.

DEVELOP PERSONAL RELATIONSHIPS

A personal relationship between executives and board members is beneficial. By knowing someone on a personal level you are better equipped to understand their areas of motivation and concern, as well as their personal style. That level of empathy translates into trust and transparency, thereby reducing the inclination to be defensive.

As you begin to get to know board members individually, you also gain an understanding of their styles and unique perspectives. When you understand what drives this person and know what they are passionate about, it enables you to relate to them in a non-defensive and empowered way. This is particularly important when there is a disagreement on an issue or a reaction such as doubt or anger. Through this personal understanding you are able to validate their perspective because you understand their unique point of view, which serves to enhance your overall effectiveness.

Remember, if you built the board with diversity, the ideas, strategies, and everything the board members bring to the table may conflict. This can be viewed as healthy if you understand where each member is coming from. Through this understanding, you know their perspective better. You can make sure you are getting everyone on the same page.

UNDERSTAND NO ONE IS ALWAYS RIGHT OR WRONG

"Board members are perfect and always right. They never make mistakes." What do you think about that statement? Hopefully, you realize that it is not true. Board members are people; therefore, they can make mistakes. When mistakes are made, the one thing a CEO should never do is make the board member feel foolish. This will solve nothing and create a new set of problems.

Even a "wrong idea" or "opinion" is considered someone's point of view. When there is a conflict on what is best for a company, the CEO should seek out understanding. Field questions to a board member that affirm the validity of what has been brought up and gain an understanding as to why that board member feels the way they do. This also presents the CEO with an opportunity to show that they are informed on the topic.

> **You do not always have to take a board members' suggestion, but you should always internalize the suggestion and determine the best course of action. Remember, board members have signed on for the job and they want to be meaningfully engaged and recognized for their contributions.**

I don't have to tell you what happens when we assume something. To avoid making assumptions you are required to do your due diligence. If you fail to communicate openly, problems will follow. In cases where you think your decision is correct—and even if it is—it will be perceived poorly if you have not communicated with the board. They will feel blindsided, which will damage the working relationship.

Take this example: A CEO may believe he has alignment around a particular acquisition at a high level. However, making that assumption that the high-level alignment is a license for the acquisition to go forward is probably a mistake. It is important for the CEO to fully educate the board on the project before he can expect to get full buy-in and move forward. You also need to strive to understand the views of the individual board members and address their concerns. Do not assume a single thing. Be in sync with all members and keep that communication open and flowing as a CEO. Use wisdom. Again, remind yourself that you have two ears and one mouth for a reason.

COMMUNICATION STANDARDS

The standards for communication are going to be based on how you structure your board. Meetings could be:

- Weekly
- Monthly

- Quarterly

A Board of Advisors has no set dates or time. The advisors set this up themselves. However, with a Board of Directors, the law (depending on the state) will require that they meet at least one time per year for a meeting. A Board of Directors meeting may also be called when momentous decisions are necessary. Many states will require that a Board of Directors meeting be announced a certain number of days in advance and may require that a board room must be used to hold a valid meeting. This can be quite the challenge, considering peoples' schedules and the potential of various locations that suit the needs for the meeting.

In addition to traditional meetings, there may be personal outreach involved. You will likely need to reach out to certain members more than others. This correspondence can take place in several forms. Email, text, or phone calls are all ways you can choose to communicate. The key is to do so in a consistent manner. This way things are not missed, and everyone understands the expectations.

Be prepared. Yes, this is more than a motto for the Boy Scouts, it is also the way business should be conducted, especially in this time where virtual meetings are so commonplace. When you are prepared, more business gets done at a higher level with better results.

When an advisor is signed on or a board member begins their term, communicating what is expected of them will be addressed. As needs may change, they should also be noted and relayed to relevant parties.

Typical expectations include:

- Bringing in funding
- Making network connections
- Arranging partnerships
- Putting together a growth strategy plan

- Other specific expectations as agreed upon by the company and advisor or board member

As mentioned, since these expectations can be adjusted and updated with time. As a member becomes more involved, for example. Perhaps someone moves from the role of advisor to that of a board member. Once everyone knows the expectations you can customize the types and methods of communication, along with frequency, to what works best for everyone.

In a typical company environment, the CEO often works with advisors on the side. Perhaps you email back and forth, maybe jump on a quick call for feedback…something like that. It is up to the CEO to use this information in a meaningful manner, if not all of it parts of it, to communicate information to the board.

Effective people are valuable because they gain perspective from other people. If a company needs a growth strategy, for example, they will approach a specific board member who has experience in this area. This person really excels at creating growth strategies that revolutionize companies.

You work to put together content and then you approach the other members of the board for feedback. As you share the premise of the content, those board members who specialize in other areas aside from growth strategy may have input. Sometimes, these can be excellent, usable ideas or they can help point out areas in the plan that need to be tightened up.

When it comes to nonprofit organizations, expectations are different. Their typical board expectation is to make a purchase to support the organization. This is their primary objective and also the reason why nonprofits usually have wealthy individuals with big checks serving on their boards. Granted, these members can provide other services that are valuable, but it is less important. Money drives nonprofits, followed by giving the organization access to a board member's network and opportunities. There is nothing wrong with this, as it meets the need. However, this need isn't part of Boardsi's primary business of creating valuable, mutually beneficial connections.

BE A GOOD ADVOCATE

One of the greatest benefits that you will bring to a board is being a good advocate. This requires clear and concise communication. Certainly not conversation that can be construed as bad. Board members promote what is great about a company, not what they personally feel is flawed or wrong. This is true of every organization, whether it is for profit or nonprofit.

There are many ways to be a good advocate for a company. We have already covered some of the basic ways to do this, such as bringing a skill or specific expertise to the table. This is so important but networking and raising money usually take the lead, especially for a new startup company.

If a startup is looking for seed investors to earn $250,000 and you're talking with them. You say you can contribute $50,000 and can also tap into your network to see what else can be raised. Your network of other executives can possibly put in the rest. Doing this will give you a seat on the board. Do you think you're going to be a positive advocate for the company, its values, vision, and mission, and overall success? You sure will be!

It may feel slightly uncomfortable, but the best advocates of a business are also the ones who set up a good business agreement to be so. Admit this and understand the reasons why it is so because it does make an impact that is associated with you. This means it should be positive! All this needs to be communicated upfront so everyone understands the expectations and hopes of the company/board relationship.

KNOW YOUR PRICE

When referring to the phrase "know your price," you likely think of these two meanings:

1. Your personal value to an organization and what it is worth
2. The amount of compensation and/or equity you are receiving for your services

By this time, you should be aware of the value you're bringing to an organization. We are going to discuss the latter right now—getting compensation and/or equity in the company. Learn what to expect, depending on what role you are serving or defining.

You are bringing the experience, expertise, wisdom, networking, and mentorship that all make for great qualities in a board member. Compared to an advisor, you have broader experience and that is what makes you set to serve the board, not act as an advisor. When serving in this capacity it is not uncommon to receive compensation for being a committee chair, for example.

Then, as a board member, you are also responsible for helping to establish the CEO's compensation. This includes defining:

- How often reviews take place for CEO
- What a reasonable pay is

What types of stocks/options are going to be made available as part of compensation

In addition, board members set the parameters for the compensation of stake holders. Their input helps to determine:

- Stock splits
- Overseeing any share purchase programs
- Approving the company's financial statements

- Recommend or discourage specific acquisitions

The communication it takes to bring all these aspects together needs to be clear and precise. Within the documents that talk about these things there is no place for speculation or opinion, just the steps that are required to be taken. You may be wondering what this really has to do with communication, and the answer is precise: The Board of Directors drives the business and is liable for certain decisions, making proper communication of ideas and policies mandatory. No exceptions!

FIND AN EFFECTIVE STRATEGY

When it comes to masterful communication you need a strategy. Most times this will mean that you are consistent in the ways you reach out to others. This means you don't randomly call one day and send a text or email the next. Be consistent and adhere to it unless everyone agrees on a different method.

The reason for consistency is that all communications should be centralized in one place and open to all board members. This makes for transparency and ease of access.

We live in a digital world now, so staying digital is my recommendation. There are great options out there for this. Boardsi is working with a company in the UK devoted to this very task. They create beneficial streams of communication for the digital world. Their platform for a central place benefits business, in general, and not just board members, alone. It's easy to log in and see what you need to see. Maybe you need to know the agenda for a meeting, as one example. Or a CEO can upload documents to share with everybody.

There are also other tools some businesses prefer, such as Google docs and Google calendar. Whatever one you choose, stick with it and be consistent. When others know where to look, they can better prepare for work on a daily basis, as well as the more intricate parts of business operations that may be duties of a board. This also extends to tasks to be completed, timelines, and "who is responsible for what" situations.

Today, there is also Zoom to consider for conversations. When holding Zoom meetings they should be recorded so the information is available to parties who may need access to it down the road.

I love meeting face-to-face primarily and have found a way to make Zoom calls be effective. This really taps into the importance of personal relationships for me. My business partners and I are effective because we know each other beyond just the scope of our work. This is significant to success because even if you don't like being face-to-face in the virtual world, you'll find that you need to be at times. It is not uncommon. You have to get over your hesitation of this and move forward. Business won't stop just because you freeze up in front of the camera.

This is the perfect time to share a bit about body language. What you do physically is a form of communication because it gives others' opportunities to perceive what you are "not saying," which does say something. The question is, what?

I have heard that 95% of communication is nonverbal. There is something about looking into someone's eyes and reading their body language. This means evaluating posture, eye contact, head tilts, and leaning in or leaning back. For me, once upon a time my nemesis was crossing my arms when I was on a video call. I had no idea that could indicate I was disinterested to somebody else. Because I wasn't so I had to correct that.

Using the 7-38-55 rule has been beneficial for me when it comes to communication and I encourage you to consider it when you evaluate your own message you send out via non-verbal communication. The breakdown is:

- 7% of communication is verbal: what are you sharing

- 55% of communication is body language: this reveals your perception of what you are sharing or hearing
- 38% of communication is the tone of voice: this clarifies and conveys the meaning of what you hear and how you respond

This translates into: Know your message. Speak clearly in a moderate tone. Be interested. And if this is not enough for you, remember the infamous and true words of Les Brown:

> "Once you open your mouth, you tell the world who you are."

VIVEKA CASE STUDY

This is the perfect case study for this chapter, as Viveka focuses on the evolution of humanity.

About Viveka
Viveka is a human growth catalyst platform designed to make transformational learning and experiences available to billions of lives around the world and amplify the evolution of humanity. The company's platform does all of the research and vetting, while connecting to sustainable and holistic methods for the organization enabling companies to increase sales revenue.

Viveka's vision is to reimagine humanity by helping individuals and companies reach their highest potential. The company has developed the world's largest and most diverse marketplace for the professional development and personal growth industry.

Overview
Viveka was looking for an executive with experience as a chief financial officer (CFO) and past involvement in initial public offering (IPO). Boardsi made an introduction with many experienced

executives and found the right hire with an impressive background. Viveka ended up hiring this executive onto their operational advisory board.

Results

Since the hire of Boardsi's recruit, Viveka is in the process of raising $50,000 of equity crowdfunding in the form of SAFE Notes via Wefunder with the goal of raising a total of $1 million. The company is also being actively tracked by PitchBook. Boardsi and Viveka continue to network and Boardsi is proud to watch the company continue to grow as they have.

Testimonial

> *"As the Founder of a fast-growing start-up, time is a limited resource and trusted advice priceless. Boardsi was recommended to us during our seed capital raise. The Boardsi team has been an invaluable counsel and presented us with great caliber advisors to support our operational advisory board. I was thoroughly impressed by the expertise, experience and network of every candidate interviewed. They allowed for a seamless process, went over and beyond to find the right candidates and were an overall joy to work with. I highly recommend Boardsi to any company seeking to expand their advisory board or board of directors."*
>
> *Katja Kempe*
> *Founder & CEO*
> *Viveka*

THE MATCHMAKER HIGHLIGHTS

Communication is one of the most important skills any person can have in their lives. Good communication is as close to a must-have quality as you will ever have. You will certainly know when you do not have it because you will spend more time cleaning up miscommunication than you will actually getting tasks done.

With the questions you will be evaluating from this chapter, I am going to request that you do a deep dive into your business life. By default, if you master communication in business, you will become more effective with it in your personal life. You'll be better all around, whether you are a CEO, board member, or both. Or if you're married, single, or a parent.

- What are my strengths in communication?
- What areas of communication should I seek improvement in?
  - How can I achieve this?
- As a CEO or board member, what is my preferred method of communication?
  - Is this true in all situations or select ones?
  - What other ways could I effectively communicate with others on key issues?
- How would I describe my tone of voice when talking to others?
- Would others agree with this assessment?
- What does my body language reveal about my perceived thoughts and responses to what others say?
  - In situations where I disagree
  - In situations where I want to learn more
  - In situations I immediately support
- How could better awareness of my body language help me in communication?
- What systems (Google docs, for example) work well with me for effective communication?

- How would I describe the flow of work with ideal communication?

As you can see, communication is the cement that holds all of our ideas, hopes, and achievements together. This means you rely on it to be solid and structured. Yet, like tie rods to give cement flexibility, you also need to be willing to adjust to best serve the needs of those you are of service to. When you do this, you are prepared to embark on a vibrant adventure that joins the best of two words: the spirit of business and the excellence of the board.

7

BUILDING BETTER FUTURES

The way to get started is to quit talking and begin doing.

WALT DISNEY

If this book has achieved its objective, it has covered valuable information on how to best run a prosperous, forward moving and thinking business. Whether you are the CEO, serving on a board or working as an advisor, or pursuing a board or advisor position, there has been information offered to help in that pursuit. This means you have:

- Unbiased outside perspectives
- Increased corporate discipline
- A keen understanding of corporate accountability and discipline
- Better prepared abilities to manage your effectiveness with CEOs and board or advisory members
- A plan (at least in the making) for showing a higher level of credibility with investors
- A customer and client-base in the business that is benefiting from the way you conduct business
- Detailed understanding of how you can benefit from others mistakes to perform your tasks more efficiently, thereby avoiding costly mistakes
- People to connect with who will round out those skills and areas of expertise which are lacking within the current management team
- A sounding board for evaluating new business ideas and opportunities
- Enhanced community and public relations
- Improved marketing results and effectiveness
- Strategic planning, assistance, and input
- Centers of influence for networking introductions
- Crisis and transition leadership at your immediate disposal
- Diversity of board, which trickles down to diversity of the organization

If you are a CEO, let me ask you: Do you have access to what is on this list?

If you are a board member the question becomes: Do you help to contribute meaningful tasks that are a part of this list?

All of these are components that a board has touches with as a company grows, adapts, and shifts to meet the demands of their customers and of the internal needs of the organization. The goal is always to learn from other people's mistakes and to have a complete skillset that is brought to life by the board, both in times of abundance and moments of crisis.

THE CRITICAL TASK

The replacement of an executive employee is one of the most pressing and important tasks that a board will have to deal with in an expedient manner, especially a CEO. Whether this person dies unexpectedly or resigns, a plan should be in place on how to handle business without them immediately. Ideally, before this person is no longer with the company.

You best handle these situations by having influence around you. This helps a board to be prepared to survive, anticipate potential market changes, and trends. COVID had provided a current and relevant example of this. When it hit, a lot of companies suffered for quite a while. Those who had a board and utilized advisors who specialized in certain areas recovered quicker. How would you be prepared to handle an unexpected turn of events that impacted the business you are associated with? Answering this question is imperative to you and your resume.

THE FACTOR OF "ADDING VALUE"

Through the collaborative efforts of a board bringing value to a CEO and organization, and the reverse—the organization providing results that drive the board, everybody is given a big opportunity to add value; value that helps build up and enhance your resume.

Being a board member is one of the most effective resume builders for CEOs and top-level executives in an organization. It takes you to the next stage of leadership, showing more than your personal accomplishments. Now you are able to share how your input and execution positively impact the ability of an organization to become better, even thrive. You do this through:

- Learning from other board members
- Taking certification courses that establish your expertise
- Having enriching life experiences
- Taking your expertise to a higher level and to other people (CFO, for example)

More often than not, if your time allows for it, once you join one board invitations to join others follow. Each time, your value and personal clout expands. It becomes an addiction of sorts because you are transitioning from being a manager of people (like a CEO) to being a leader. There is a distinct difference.

ROBUST RESULTS

If you had a choice of either robust or just bust, which one would you pick? I am going to guess robust! Having a board to help you excel in all areas of your company will lead to the robust results that define your business and your success within the industry you are in.

If a company has outstanding services or amazing products, but lacks growth and branding, they will not perform to their best ability. Key additions of the right people to serve on a board or act in an advisory capacity can set the tone for the company's ultimate success. If a company had an amazing service, perhaps something with AI technology, does it also have the experience and expertise to bring it to the right customer. Once upon a time, it was a common problem to have a unique and great product, such as an AI one, and not have the tools to get it to market. Similar challenges still exist today. The prepared company circumvents these roadblocks and business obstacles by having the right team in place, from the top down.

One of the most exciting aspects of my work is to see how companies learn to effectively use their board and advisors to do incredible things. A company that is bought for pennies on the dollar can bring in a group of people that take the business to the next level. They make it a big deal by bringing on the board that knows how to lead others effectively, leaving no room for a company to self-manage. These are individuals who know how to inspire others to generate results. I love to meet these people and am fortunate to get to on a daily basis!

COMMUNITY INVOLVEMENT

Most every business is a part of the community in which their headquarters are, at minimum. The people who work for the organization live in these communities and contribute in various ways. Perhaps they coach their kid's softball team, or they volunteer. Often times, you will see that these wonderful contributors are actually board members and executives. They understand how valuable the connection is to them and they value making new connections.

Community also comes into play for the product or service you offer, depending on what it is. Today, companies can no longer afford to overlook the communities they are in. The right board can help them to maximize this relationship, so everyone benefits, including those who are a part of the expanded community. The expanded community is the talent pool you can bring to your board from areas that are typically a further distance away than what a person would drive from daily. This is one of the greatest benefits of video conferencing and businesses that use this tool the right way also expands their community at the same time.

At Boardsi, community involvement means a lot. In the towns we are already established, we bring this to our communities:

- Our tax dollars
- Involvement in nonprofits
- Encouraging employee involvement in the community at all levels

When you build a board with the right people, these people will bring fresh ideas on how to enrich a community and can benefit from doing so.

Here is something we recently did to stay involved in the community. I have a passion for soccer, coached competitive soccer for both of my kids since they were 5 and until they graduated High School. No more hands-on coaching but we have the ability to help in other ways. Here is the Press Release:

Boardsi PARTNERS WITH THE SAN FRANCISCO NIGHTHAWKS

"After coaching girls and boy's competitive soccer for more than 15 years, this partnership only made sense," said Martin Rowinski, Boardsi CEO. "I love the mission of the SF Nighthawks and what they stand for. Seeing the team get great exposure and the opportunity to continue to play professional soccer all over the world is something that myself and Boardsi want to continue to support."

Boardsi will sponsor the team by helping offset costs and securing community outreach, which both enable athletes to play on the team for free. Doing this provides a safe platform for a variety of skilled players to advance to college and professional soccer careers or continue to play with the Nighthawks post-graduation.

"We want to thank Boardsi for recognizing in us Kindred Spirits," said Jill Lounsbury, San Francisco Nighthawks General Manager. "We look forward to growing this relationship to afford more players the opportunity to play at the highest level. A frequently overlooked fact is that 80% of women CEOs played NCAA athletics, and 95% of high school and college players who play with us become captains of their college teams. With Boardsi's help we are helping to create the CEOs of the future!"

The San Francisco Nighthawks were founded in 1995 with the goal to elevate and promote the Women's Soccer game and to provide the highest opportunity to Bay Area players. The organization's belief is that every female player, who is qualified to play at this high level, should be afforded the opportunity to play with the Nighthawks regardless of age, physical size, race, preferences, identities, socio-economic background, education, or previous club. Boardsi is a strong believer in diversity within organizations and communities and is committed to supporting the San Francisco Nighthawks and their endeavors to empower female players and provide them with tremendous opportunities on and off the field.

The Nighthawk's motto is, "We are more than just the 90 minutes we play on the field. As our Nighthawks' network of social justice advocates enter the mainstream workforce it is our desire to elevate women's voices, amplify social causes such as

Racial Justice, Women's Rights, LGBTQ+ Rights, Children's Rights, and speak for those that might not have a seat at the table. We have partnered in the past with many local Youth Clubs and will continue to do so."

Boardsi is thrilled to support the SF Nighthawks and couldn't agree more with their saying, "All help is good help. We are stronger together."

Learn more about the San Francisco Nighthawks: https://www.sfnighthawks.com/

> "The value of a man resides in what he gives and not in what he is capable of receiving."
> -Albert Einstein

Another important note about the community and the company connection is that through your involvement with the community you have a chance to demonstrate how you are a business that adheres to your values, vision, and mission. This is an action that people take note of; the type where someone can confidently say, "They do what they say they're going to do."

THE VALUE, VISION, AND MISSION ARE CLEARLY KNOWN

I've already talked (probably too much) about how every person that is a part of a business culture should have a clear understanding of the company's value, vision, and mission. The board helps ensure this is in place and being acted upon always. A board will also ensure that these items are at the core of any decisions being made on the business's behalf.

Companies who reach this stage are not focused on just producing a product that sells, alone. They realize that the talent they bring to their board will connect the dots that make for a complete picture. These organizations go to a higher level. We saw this play out brilliantly with one former CEO. He joined a board for a new company with a new type of product for the market. The company's primary owner thought success would be getting the product into stores for sale and on Amazon. That would be successful but with the vision of the CEO we connected the company with, they were able to expand to a massive deal that included placing this product in hotel rooms for a major chain, as well. Even some cruise ships too! The success of this story is a perfect example of how amazing the results can be when a board helps to connect the dots.

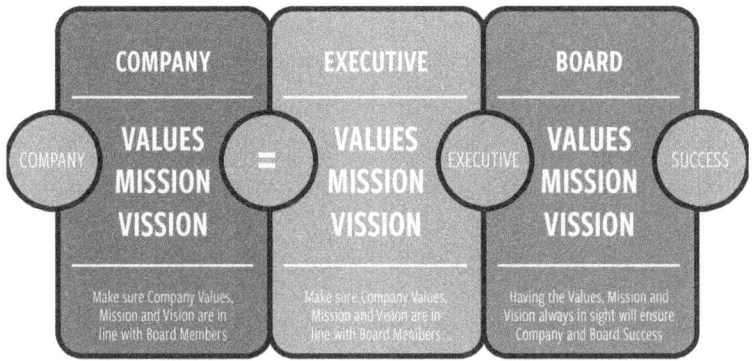

A CASE STUDY FOR A FINTECH IPO

This company's name is being held per company request, as they are preparing for a future IPO.

About Fintech Company, Inc.
Fintech Company, Inc. is a payment solutions platform that gives customers and merchants the ability to use digital payments and loyalty programs. Can you dream of a world where you aren't fumbling with your wallet and searching for the right credit card, loyalty card, or coupon? That is what Fintech Company, Inc. has found a solution for. An easy-to-use solution that works by

simply tapping your screen or passing your phone near a checkout terminal.

Overview

Fintech Company, Inc. teamed up with Boardsi to help them build their board. The company was searching for experienced executives to help increase their reach and diversify their board. After a few months of interviews, Fintech Company, Inc. hired Boardsi recruits Robin Meister and Lynn Perkins to join their Board of Directors team.

Results

Fintech Company, Inc. was able to get two of the board members that they needed based on the skill sets that they were looking for with a very quick turnaround. The board members that were recruited met all the expectations that they were looking for and checked all the diversity boxes. The executives that they hired not only will help with the direction of the company but will also be able to open up the doors that they need opened to get to the next level.

Testimonial

> "While looking at adding new board members one thing that was universal amongst our members was the need and want to make our board more diversified. It is difficult to advertise for what it was we were looking for, but Boardsi made it quite easy and simple. We gave Boardsi about 20 different skill sets and data points we were looking for in the board members we wanted to explore, and they were able to match pretty much all of the different things we were looking for. Boardsi was able to take what we were looking for and instead of us having to search through the small pool that we have always looked through they were able to get us in

front of the masses and in turn provided us with the specifics we were looking for. If you think you need to explore the possibilities of a board or advisors in your organization, you are right and Boardsi is the place not just to look but to find what your perfect match."

CEO
Fintech Company, Inc.

THE MATCHMAKER HIGHLIGHTS

Our world is comprised of communities. They are everywhere, from where we live locally to the expansion of our work community, which can be global. Whatever it is, we should treat it with the reverence it deserves and play our parts to ensure we are giving our best.

For businesses, their boards play an intricate role in creating a robust relationship that is good for all it connects with. When all works together as it should, the magic of the relationship is undeniable.

The questions below are excellent information to help guide you to the robust future you desire for your company and/or with your role as a board member or advisor for an organization. When these questions are taken to heart, successful leaders emerge. When leaders succeed, the people they are guiding succeed too.

What are my best ways to receive an unbiased outside perspective that will be beneficial to my company?

- What do I enjoy about being disciplined and held accountable for my choices?
- How can I benefit the community I live in best?
    - Why is community important to me?

- What roles am I suited to play that will enhance my company's outcome, either as an executive or a board member?
- How am I most effective in my role right now?
  - What are my goals that still need to be developed?
  - What is my plan to achieve these goals?
- How do my customers benefit from the way I conduct business? (If you are a board member the customer is the company; if you are a CEO, the customer is your employees)
- How do I gain credibility with investors?
- Who do I have to turn to as a sounding board for business plans and ideas?
  - How are these individuals effective in helping me?
  - How could these dynamics be improved?
- In what ways do I live out my company's values?
- In what ways do I contribute to my company's mission?
- How do I view my company's vision?
- In what ways am I committed to having a diverse board?

These questions will help you to reveal the fullest and best potential of your organization and the board that drives it. This will help to identify the person you are and the example you set for others. If people are always watching, let them watch a great example!

THE MATCHMAKER'S INVITATION

What you choose to talk about is only a dream. After you envision it, it becomes possible. But only when you schedule it in does it become one hundred percent real.

MARTIN ROWINSKI

If you want to make sure you're doing business the right way, write a book and you'll get a chance to find out. Throughout each of these chapters and the case studies, I have put myself in situations where I had to evaluate every detail of what we do at Boardsi and find a way to express the individual accountability component of it too. This made the journey of creating this book both therapeutic and beneficial.

As we continue to thrive and help companies achieve their goals and visions, we rely on people like you—executives and maybe even current board members who want to become a part of a business's solution for prosperity. One thing for certain is that what we do at Boardsi has made a positive impact, and I am grateful for it. Being the matchmaker between companies and those individuals who can best serve them through a board role or an advisory position, is more than a goal, it's a passion that I have, and the entire organization has, as well.

Whether you are a CEO looking for board members or an executive looking to join a board, these words were all put together with one hope: To benefit you and help you expand your thoughts to the positive impact you could have and the serious commitment that it involves. Are you ready to be a part of the solution? Because regardless of who you are, the right board for an organization delivers benefits that go beyond what you may envision alone. If it is a team effort, you want a stellar team!

CHALLENGE YOURSELF

Taking on a job isn't always easy. There can be challenges and that is brilliant. I find a daily challenge, whether large or small, to be a necessity to the lifelong pursuit of growth and development. This is why every day I challenge myself to do something that's new or something I was maybe scared to do a year ago. Just starting Boardsi is testament to that. Before it took off, it felt like a massive task. Let's be real, it is a massive task, but it has immense rewards that make everything the Boardsi team and I do worth it. Through the importance of creating these executive/board connections, I continue to explore my life, motives, and reasons more thoroughly, so they benefit you the way I have experienced their benefits. If committed to the process, you can expect to do this too.

If you are an advisor for an organization, understand what you can do. Use the network to develop what you are there for. Use your knowledge and accept challenges for growth. Feed off other advisors to become better. Become a part of the process and the results will be that you enrich others' lives, not just your own. You are a key contributor to people recognizing their value and the result is rewarding experiences that everyone can benefit from. Whether they serve on one board or several, this is true.

Whether you are in your thirties or forties, it is time to evaluate the success you've had and how serving as an advisor or board member could add to it. Even if you're retired, you still have experience and expertise that could serve others well. Don't let your mind die; stay active. Being on a board is one way to do just that! It gives you the opportunity to still use your talents and meet new people and develop new networks.

When you build a Board of Directors or Advisors you are contributing value to an organization. Your time and effort matter. Whether you are seeking the outside perspective or are the outside perspective seeking a position, it is the start of an important union that will enhance your life and your professional relationships. Sometimes, these people do not come along right away, which is why Boardsi is a great ally in the hunt for them.

Boardsi flourishes when we help individuals match up with organizations in which they share the same values, vision, and mission. A company could have a board that's half full and the next thing you know, it could be overflowing with the productive abundance that comes from real contributors to a company and its purpose.

Board members are involved individuals who are positive forces for good in their work and in their communities. They bring their value to others through effective leadership and a commitment to the overall vision.

A STARTING POINT FROM THE CORPORATE MATCHMAKER

If you are at the start of building up your board credentials, why not start local. Serve on a nonprofit board. A great example of this would be a board for a sports organization. Think of how many parents are working several jobs and cannot afford to pay for their child to play sports. You can use your skills in fundraising to create the financial means for these kids to play in the sports. This can help to bring a positive and fun influence on these kids' lives—a defining moment!

Use this experience to build up your abilities and prepare yourself to become as certified as you can in order to prepare for serving on a board someday. It is never too early—or too late—to do this.

What ideas do you have? Pull out your Corporate Matchmaker Journal and start writing them down. If you only have a moment, start by writing the broad idea down and then go back later and start writing out your thoughts, ideas, and plans in greater detail. Doing these small steps is the starting point and it plants the seed for massive action. Through personal growth, development, and initiatives you provide the water that brings life to what you've put into motion.

I also would love to be a part of this process and encourage you to reach out to me with questions and ideas. Here's where you can connect with me:

LinkedIn: https://www.linkedin.com/in/martinrowinski/
Website: https://boardsi.com or https://martinrowinski.com

As we create these connections, great things will unfold. I feel sure of it. The words of Mahatma Gandhi state it well:

> "The best way to find yourself is to lose yourself in the service of others."

Much thanks to you.
Martin

> **"We must give more in order to get more. It is the generous giving of we that produces the generous harvest."**
> Orison Swett Marden

RECOMMENDED RESOURCES

ONE GOAL.
CONNECT EXECUTIVES WITH COMPANIES.

Boardsi matches executives with Board Positions:

- Board of Directors
- Board of Advisors

Executives join Boardsi private network to learn more about opprtunities.
Companies connect with Boardsi to find TOP-TALENT

Join Boardsi at boardsi.com

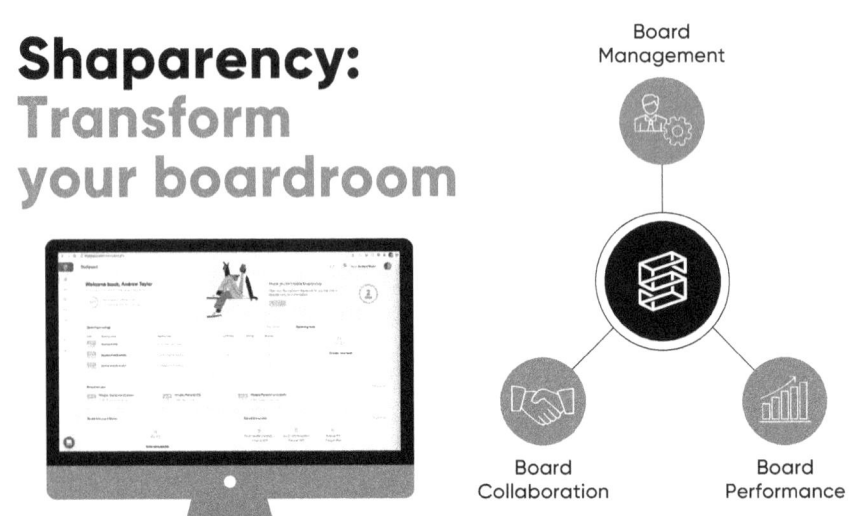

Shaparency:
Transform your boardroom

Board Management

Board Collaboration

Board Performance

www.shaparency.com

www.ingramcontent.com/pod-product-compliance
Lightning Source LLC
Chambersburg PA
CBHW032047150426
43194CB00006B/448